SHARMIN MOSSAVAR-RAHMANI

BOND INDEX FUNDS

PROBUS PUBLISHING COMPANY
Chicago, Illinois

Library of Congress Cataloging in Publication Data Available

ISBN 1-55738-014-7

Printed in the United States of America

1 2 3 4 5 6 7 8 9 0

Contents

Preface

On joining Wall Street several years ago, first on the sell-side and later on the buy-side, I stumbled into the then-obscure niche of fixed income market indexes. At the time, very little research was publicly circulated—if it existed at all—covering the construction and design of indexes, the replicability of index returns or the methodology for tracking indexes. The Salomon Brothers Long-Term High-Grade Corporate Bond Index was the primary performance bogey for bond managers, and the Lehman Brothers Kuhn Loeb Government/Corporate Index was gaining followers as a more appropriate—and easier to outperform—benchmark. Later, despite the creation of hundreds of indexes and billions of dollars in indexed assets, new fixed income analysts continued to face a dearth of available information. I took to filling that gap, at least partially, by publishing articles on indexing fixed income assets and on designing customized benchmarks. Those articles became the starting point for this book.

Bond Index Funds provides plan sponsors and consultants with a review of the role of such funds, particularly enhanced index funds, in an overall investment policy. It is also intended as a guide for plan sponsors to selecting an index fund advisor from among what often is perceived to be a homogeneous group. New entrants to the fixed income market can use this book to gain quick understanding of different indexes and the investment strategies used to outperform them. In addition, I have tried to alert the fixed income community to the implications of increased use of indexing for the fixed income market. These include the inevitable and early consolidation in the investment advisory community and declining profit margins.

Frank J. Fabozzi encouraged me to publish the early series of articles and continued to support me with his usual good humor as I completed this book. I would also like to acknowledge the assistance of colleagues at Fidelity and of analysts at Wall Street firms who provided invaluable data. Finally, my husband, Bijan, provided many helpful suggestions and endless editorial improvements. I thank them all.

Sharmin Mossavar-Rahmani

Introduction

During the 1980's, assets invested in bond and equity index funds jumped from only several hundred million dollars to over $250 billion—and the volume is still growing. Of the total, about one-third currently is committed to U.S. investment-grade bond index funds. Investors in bond index funds include public, corporate and multiple employer pension plans, endowments, insurance companies, liability reserve funds, and individual investors in mutual funds. Their assets are managed to match or slightly outperform a particular domestic or international bond index.

To take advantage of the rapidly rising interest in bond indexing, key Wall Street broker/dealers have introduced dozens of bond indexes, notably such broad market benchmarks as the Salomon Brothers Broad Investment-Grade Bond Index and the Lehman Brothers Aggregate Index, such market subsector benchmarks as the Morgan Stanley Actively Traded Mortgage-Backed Securities Index, and such specialized benchmarks as the Merrill Lynch Treasury Strips Index.

Growth in bond index funds also has triggered an increase in the number of investment advisors providing index fund management services from less than a handful in 1980 to nearly 50 by 1990. In addition, several pension plan sponsors manage bond index funds within their own organizations rather than retain outside investment advisors.

Yet despite increased use, bond indexing is little understood. Skeptics allege that bond indexing offers, at best, mediocre or average total return performance. As shown in Chapter I, among a universe of active fixed income investment advisors, bond index funds typically produce above average returns over a market cycle and often rank above the 25th percentile. In addition, studies on the consistency of active fixed income advisors have shown that less than one percent of such advisors have outperformed the Salomon Brothers Broad Investment-Grade Bond Index every year for the 10-year period ending in 1989.

The management of bond index funds also has been described as "computer-driven," "mindless," "faceless," and even "easy," requiring indexing software but little investment expertise. While such characteristics may describe certain types of equity indexing, bond index fund management is, in reality, technically difficult. Understanding the design and underlying assumptions of bond indexes requires a thorough knowledge of fixed income securities and their cash flow structures, embedded options, and reinvestment rates. So, too, does gauging the impact of different designs and underlying assumptions on total returns. The design and assumptions underlying key bond indexes are described in Chapter II.

Similarly, technical and investment expertise are required for the selection of the appropriate indexing technique to set up and manage each type and size of index fund. Unlike most equity index funds, bond index funds cannot match the performance of their benchmark simply by purchasing a pro rata share of all securities in the index. Index fund advisors must utilize sophisticated indexing techniques outlined in Chapter III to set up a portfolio with the targeted risk and return characteristics; they then must rely on their investment expertise to select specific securities from among literally thousands of issues available in the fixed income market.

Bond indexing has been equated erroneously with "passivity" and index fund advisors with "robot investors." Traditionally, the term "passive" or "structured" fixed income management has been used to describe investment styles that closely track a benchmark; e.g., an index or a liability schedule. Indexing, immunization and dedication are such investment styles. The term "active" has been used to describe fixed income investment styles that depend heavily on forecasting of short- and long-term interest rates. The nomenclature notwithstanding, managing bond index funds is far from passive. Keeping the risk and return characteristics of a bond index fund in line with those of its benchmark, monitoring credit quality of securities, offsetting transaction costs of bond index funds, reinvesting cash flows generated by the portfolio, and minimizing tracking error (Chapter IV) are labor-intensive and demand active involvement and risky decisions on the part of index fund advisors. Many bond index funds are managed as enhanced index funds. Index fund advisors enhance the total return of such funds by employing the same investment strategies used by traditional active investment advisors. However, unlike traditional active investment advisors, bond index fund advisors implement these strategies while maintaining the same effective (also referred to as "call-adjusted" or "option-adjusted") duration as that of the benchmark. As illustrated in Chapter V, understanding and successfully implementing these strategies and correctly assessing their risk and return trade-offs require active participation of bond index fund advisors.

Proliferation of bond indexing will continue to shape the fixed income market. Profit margins throughout the investment community will shrink: investment advisors will be forced to accept lower fees, financial consultants will be retained less frequently and broker/dealers will face lower bid-ask price spreads. In addition, with lower turnover of bond index funds, short-term market volatility and trading volume will decline, further squeezing the broker/dealer community.

Increased bond indexing will lead also to a shake-out within the investment advisory community; given greater control and predictability of bond index funds, investors commit much larger assets to a single bond index fund advisor than they would to any single traditional active investment advisor. Already, only five fixed income advisors manage about 60 percent of all assets placed in bond index funds. These and other consequences of increased indexing are described in Chapter VI.

Will the dramatic growth in bond indexing be sustained in the 1990's? The answer is yes, barring a major shift of assets away from the fixed income sector generally. And a greater share of assets attracted to bond index funds will be directed to enhanced and customized funds.

The continued growth of bond indexing will be sustained by two factors: performance and level of investor control of fixed income assets. Indexing is likely to continue providing better performance than the performance offered by traditional active management. Adding value in the fixed income market has become increasingly difficult. Investment advisors are more sophisticated, broker/dealers have entire trading desks dedicated to taking advantage of arbitrage opportunities, quantitative and credit research analysis are widely used, and extensive information systems instantaneously transmit data to the investment community. Market sectors are evaluated constantly and securities have become more efficiently priced. Hundreds of market participants monitor the markets with "Star Wars" systems to capitalize on the smallest arbitrage, thereby preventing sectors and securities from getting out of line for any period of time. In such competitive and complex markets, pension plan sponsors and other investors will recognize the low likelihood of consistently obtaining value above an enhanced bond index fund through traditional active management. Investors will turn instead to indexing.

In addition to improved relative performance, indexing offers investors a mechanism to exercise greater control over their fixed income assets. Historically, the role of fixed income assets in a typical portfolio was one of diversification. Today, diversification can be achieved through investments in real estate, foreign securities, venture capital and leveraged buy-out funds, among others. Fixed income assets, therefore, can be used to accomplish additional investment objectives beyond diversification, notably by providing a predictable stream of cash flows or, at times, by serving as a deflationary hedge for the entire portfolio. Indeed, in pursuit of such objectives, many investors have been articulating very specific risk and return parameters for their fixed income assets. To ensure that their fixed income advisors do not deviate from those parameters, investors turn to bond index funds. For example, selection of a particular long- duration index fund assures the investor that fixed income assets provide the deflationary hedge commensurate with that long duration. Allowing a traditional active investment advisor to control the duration of the fixed income assets is less reliable. If his timing is off, he may opt for a short duration as interest rates fall and, thereby, fail to provide the desired hedge in a deflationary interest rate environment.

More and more, actively-managed bond portfolios will be transformed into a variety of bond index funds. As the shift occurs, the investment community will be faced with several decisions. Investors who do not use bond index funds will examine the advantages and disadvantages of indexing; should they decide not to index part of their fixed income assets, they will be required to formulate thorough and well-documented arguments for selecting alternative investment styles. And those who decide to invest in bond index funds will need to choose between internal and external management of indexed assets.

A critical issue facing fixed income investment advisors—traditional, active advisors as well as those managing index funds or other quantitative strategies—is how to survive and capitalize on the coming shake-out in the investment advisory community. Many traditional active investment advisors will be pressured to offer index fund management capabilities, because most successful fixed income advisors in the United States—those with both significant assets under management and highly regarded investment expertise—offer some type of index fund management capability. Meanwhile, index fund advisors will be preparing for a period of intense competition. One approach—an expensive one—to preparing for such competition will be to complement investment expertise in different market sectors with state-of-the-art information systems, extensive credit and quantitative research skills, and analytical systems that help measure and explain the value added by the index fund advisors. Overcoming the drawbacks of the current analytical systems, notably pricing, modeling of complex securities, and performance attribution are key to such an approach.

The shift into bond index funds will present the broker/dealer community with challenges as well. The number of large-volume, one-shot transactions will increase as investors shift assets away from actively-managed portfolios. Capturing a significant share of these transactions, especially given low turnover of assets once a bond index fund is in place, will be important to the profitability of broker/dealers. Additional trading volume then can be generated by focusing on index fund investors who manage their fixed income assets internally. Such investors do not have the extensive resources available at the large investment advisory firms. They will look to broker/dealers for research support and recommendations for rebalancing their index funds, and, in return, will direct trades to those broker/dealers.

The days of easy money in the fixed income market appear to be over. Assets under management are not increasing as rapidly as they did in the 1980's when the increase in assets under management was fueled by the tremendous growth of pension funds. Already, advisory fees are shrinking. Broker/dealers no longer can command the wide bid-ask spreads of the past. Investment advisors cannot add significant and sustainable value as readily by discovering neglected and hence undervalued securities. This increasingly difficult fixed income environment notwithstanding, the role—and impact—of bond index funds will grow. The purpose of this book is to explore the dynamics of that growth, comparing the benefits and shortcomings of bond index funds, examining alternative benchmarks and investment techniques, proposing strategies to enhance returns, and describing the implications of the spread of indexing for the fixed income market.

Chapter 1

Indexing: Advantages and Disadvantages

Since it was first introduced in 1979, fixed income indexing has attracted a diverse group of investors. Some of the nation's largest pension plan sponsors, universities, foundations, and insurance companies have indexed a significant portion, if not all, of their fixed income assets. Among public funds, the entire $17 billion comprising fixed income assets of the New York City Retirement System has been indexed. In the corporate sector, American Telephone and Telegraph Co. has indexed as much as $3.5 billion. Other large institutions that have indexed a portion of their fixed income assets include Exxon Corporation, CBS Inc., and the Rockefeller Foundation.

These investors have been motivated to index fixed income assets by some combination of the following factors: improved performance relative to active management; lower advisory fees relative to active management; lower non-advisory-fee expenses associated with hiring investment advisors; shift in control of investments away from investment advisors into the hands of investors; and the greater ability to measure value added by investment advisors.

ADVANTAGES

Performance

The most important motivating factor to drive indexing has been the poor and inconsistent performance of active investment advisors. In past years, the returns of most active investment advisors have lagged the returns of market indexes. In addition, active investment advisors who have matched or outperformed market indexes only have done so inconsistently when measured over ten-year periods. Investors, therefore, have turned to index funds to obtain both higher long-term returns as well as more consistent and reliable short-term performance.

Exhibit 1-1 compares the annualized returns of active investment advisors with the returns of a widely-used market index for one-, three-, five-, and ten-year periods ending December 1989.[1] (One-, three-, five-, and ten-year periods are used commonly to evaluate the performance of investment advisors.) In all four periods, the market returns—represented by the Salomon Brothers Broad Investment-Grade Bond Index (Salomon BIG Index)—were higher than the returns of the median active investment advisor. In three of the four periods, market index returns ranked above or as high as the 25th percentile level of active investment advisors; in other words, three-quarters of active investment advisors underperformed the market index. For the ten-year period ending December 1989, the market index returns ranked at the 19th percentile level.

Exhibit 1-2 compares the returns of active investment advisors with the returns of the market index for each year between 1977[2] and 1989. The median active investment advisor outperformed the market index in only five of those 13 years—1977, 1978, 1979, 1981,

1. Active investment advisors have been ranked by their total return, as measured by the consultants SEI Funds Evaluation Services. The rankings are segmented into the fifth, 25th, 50th (or median), 75th, and 95th percentile levels. Market returns are represented by the Salomon Brothers Broad Investment-Grade Bond Index since the latter is among the most widely used broad market benchmarks for measuring performance of active investment advisors.

2. 1977 is the earliest year for which broad market index data is available.

Exhibit 1-1. Annualized Total Return For Fixed Income Funds (For Periods Ending December 31, 1989)

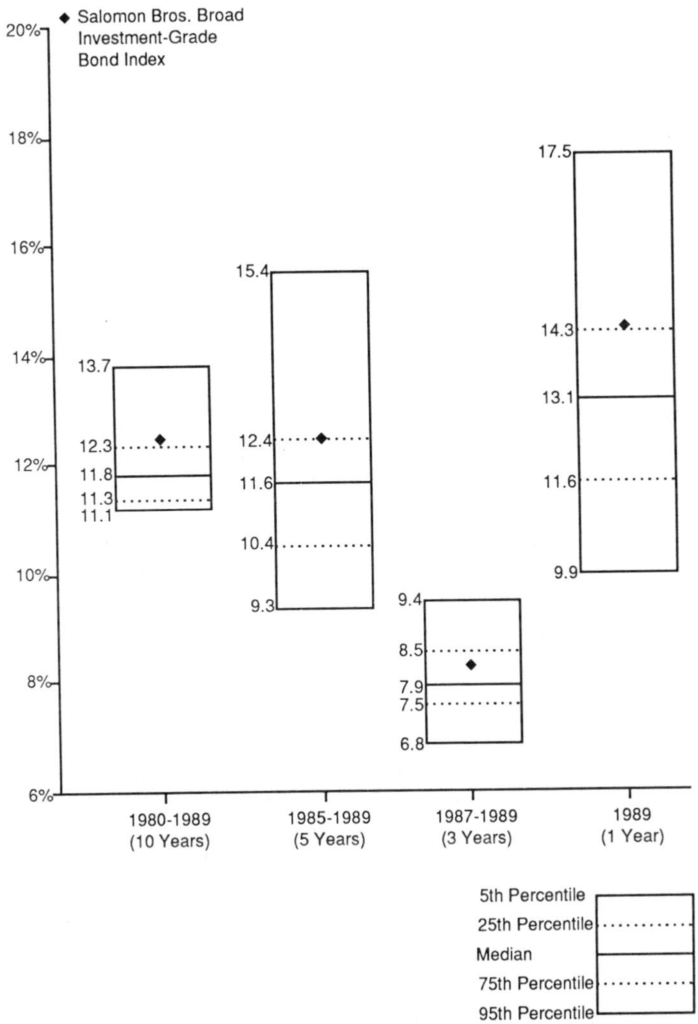

Source: SEI Corporation.

Exhibit 1-2. Annualized Total Return For Fixed Income Funds (For Years Ending December 31, 1989)

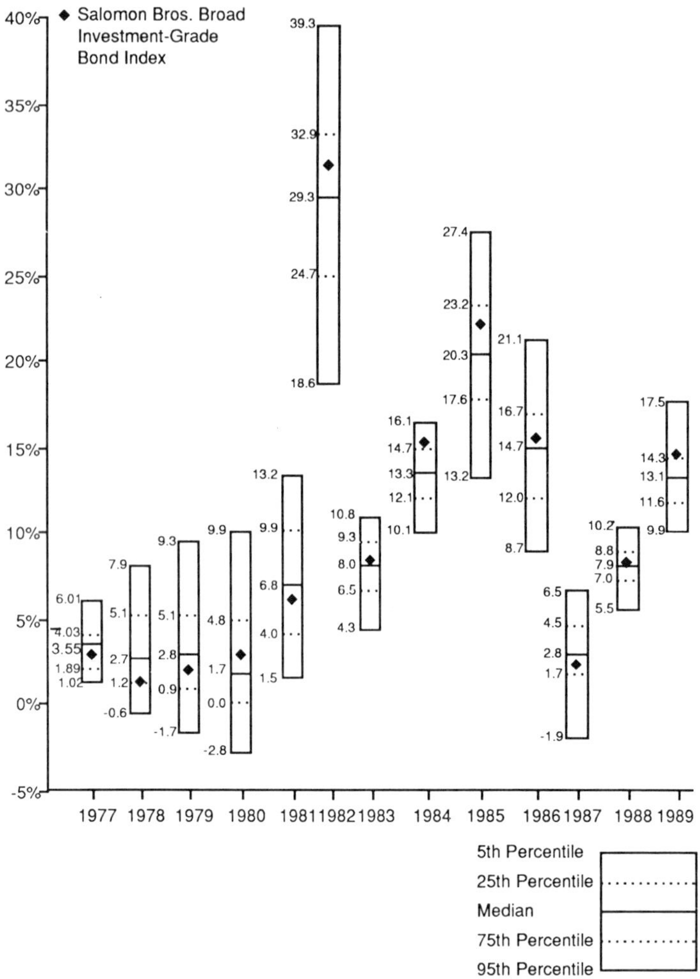

*The Lehman Brothers Aggregate Index was used for time periods prior to 1980 because of lack of data on Salomon Index.

Source: SEI Corporation.

and 1987, each of which was characterized by rising interest rates. Of the remaining eight years, the median active investment advisor nearly matched the market index in only one year—1983—and significantly underperformed in index in four years—1982, 1984, 1985, and 1989, all of which represented periods of falling interest rates. In 1984, as many as 79 percent of active investment advisors underperformed the market index.

The performance of active investment advisors during these years was not only poor, it was also inconsistent. Even those active investment advisors whose ten-year returns ranked above the 25th percentile did not rank consistently above the 25th percentile on a year-by-year basis. Furthermore, very few active investment advisors consistently ranked above the market index on a year-by-year basis. Finally, active investment advisors who outperformed the market index in periods of rising rates underperformed it in periods of falling rates.

Exhibits 1-3 and 1-4 summarize some of the results of a study conducted by SEI Corporation on the consistency of performance of active investment advisors between 1980 and 1989. Exhibit 1-3 shows the percentage of active fixed income investment advisors who outperformed the Salomon BIG Index for a given number of years between 1980 and 1989. For example, the first bar (from left) indicates that not even 0.5 percent of active advisors outperformed the Salomon BIG Index in each of the ten years ending with 1989. Only 2.4 percent outperformed the index in nine of the 10 years ending 1989. The last bar indicates that all active investment advisors succeeded in outperforming the index at least once over the ten-year period. The sum of the first five bars indicate that only 30.1 percent of all active investment advisors outperformed the index in at least six of the 10 years ending 1989.

Exhibit 1-4 shows the percentage of active fixed income advisors who outperformed the median investment advisor for a given number of years between 1980 and 1989. The data shows that only 1.2 percent of active investment advisors outperformed the median investment advisor in each of the 10 years. Furthermore, only 37.2 percent outperformed the median investment advisor in at least five of the 10 years. Active investment advisors not only un-

Exhibit 1-3. Percent of Fixed Income Funds Consistently Above Salomon Brothers Broad Investment-Grade Bond Index (Annual Periods through December 31, 1989)

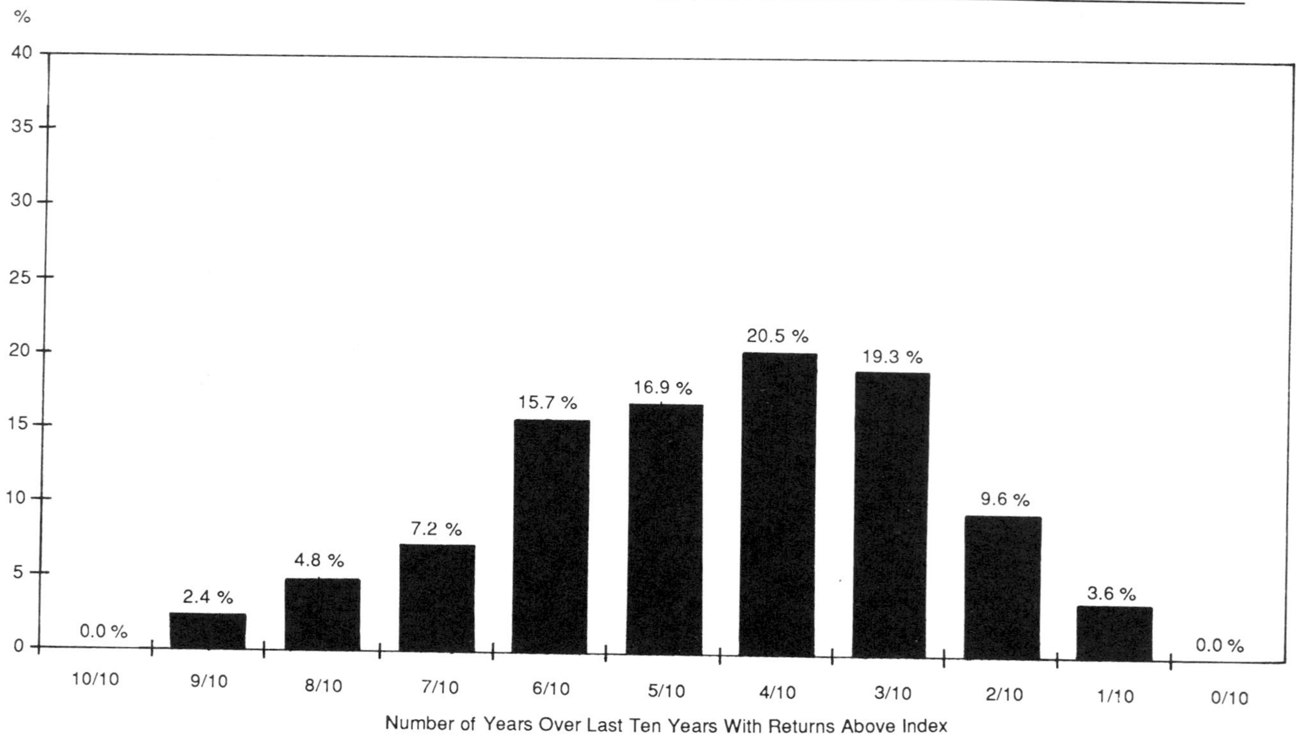

Source: SEI Corporation.

Exhibit 1-4. Percent of Fixed Income Funds Consistently Above Median (Annual Periods through December 31, 1989)

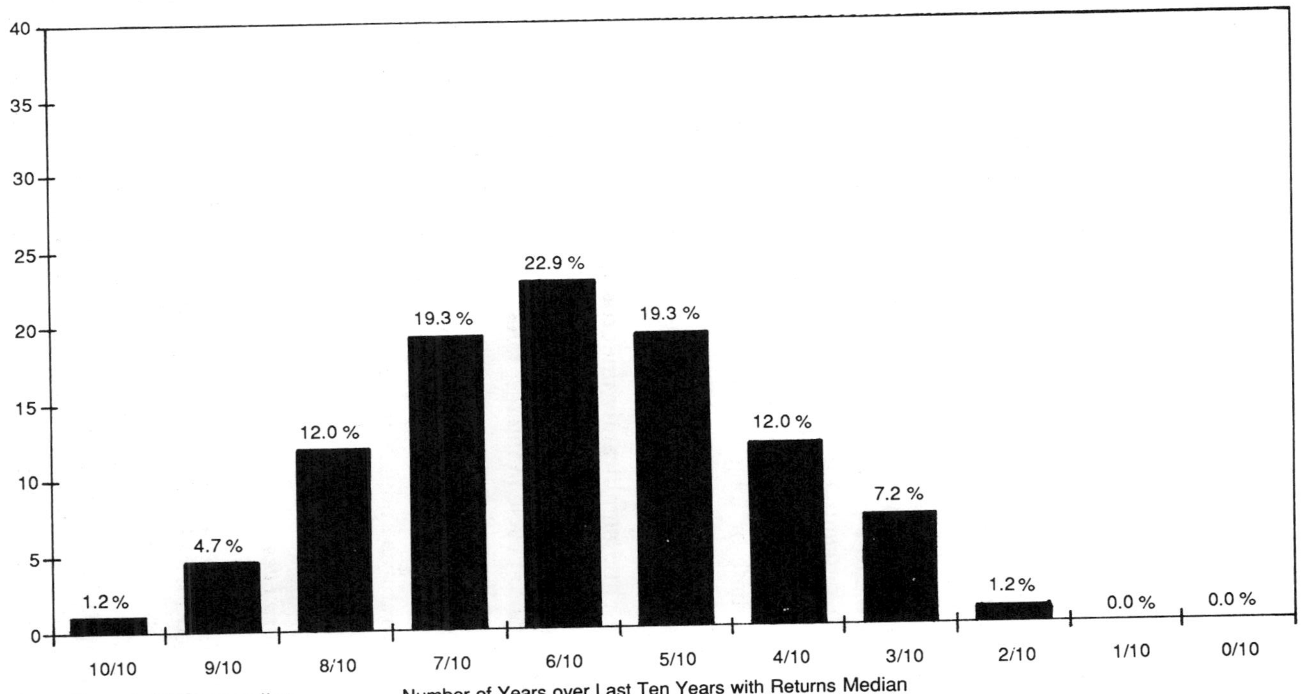

Source: SEI Corporation.

derperformed the market index, but they also failed to outperform the median investment advisor consistently.

Finally, active investment advisors have inconsistent rankings in different interest rate environments. More than half of active investment advisors whose returns ranked above the 25th percentile in a period of rising rates produced returns below the 75th percentile in the subsequent period of falling rates. Similarly, more than half of active investment advisors whose returns ranked below the 75th percentile in a period of rising rates produced returns above the 25th percentile in the subsequent period of falling rates. These reversals in ranking can be explained by management style of those active investment advisors who specialize in securities with either intermediate or long terms-to-maturity. For example, an active investment advisor who specializes in securities with long terms-to-maturity (commonly referred to as a long bond manager) will outperform most performance benchmarks in a period of falling interest rates, and significantly underperform in a period of rising rates. Therefore, an investor hiring such an active investment advisor will experience inconsistent performance rankings of assets over a complete market cycle in interest rates.

The limited success of active investment advisors who systematically outperform both the market index and the median investment advisor thus has prompted investors to turn to indexing for higher returns and a more reliable alternative to active fixed income investment management.

Advisory Fees

Another key advantage of indexing is the lower advisory fees charged for index fund management relative to the fees charged for active investment management. Advisory fees for index funds range from 30 to 75 percent of the advisory fees charged for actively-managed portfolios. Advisory fees for a $50 million actively-managed portfolio typically range between 20 and 40 basis points (or between 0.20 and 0.40 percent of the market value of the portfolio). Fees for a $50 million index fund typically range from five to 17 basis points.

The highest fees, about 20 basis points, are charged for enhanced or customized index funds (see Chapters 3 and 5), and significantly lower fees—a mere one or two basis points—are charged for very large index funds (say, in excess of $1 billion). The savings in advisory fees from indexing, therefore, can be substantial, particularly in the case of large funds.

Advisory fees for index funds and actively-managed portfolios differ depending not only on the size of the assets being managed, but also on the type of organization managing the assets. In general, investment advisory firms charge higher fees than insurance companies, which in turn charge higher fees than bank trust departments. And in all three types of organizations, smaller accounts are charged higher fees than large accounts. Exhibit 1-5 summarizes average advisory fees reported to have been charged for active management. Comparable data for index fund management is not available.

It should be noted that data on advisory fees is limited and sometimes unreliable. Advisory fee schedules provided by investment advisors do not always reflect the fees eventually charged to the investor. For example, public pension plan sponsors and Taft-Hartley (or jointly-trusteed, multiple-employer) plan sponsors often negotiate lower advisory fees, particularly when portfolios are larger than $50 million. Also, investment advisors are reluctant to

Exhibit 1.5. Fixed Income Advisory Fees in Basis Points as of December 1988

Range of Fee\Account Size ($ Million)

	$50-74	*74-99*	*100-199*	*200-299*	*300+*
Highest	38	31	30	26	27
25th Percentile	29	27	25	22	18
Median	27	25	20	15	12
75th Percentile	22	20	16	9	5
Lowest	13	10	11	6	1

Source: SEI Corporation.

provide fee data that may be lower than published industry advisory fees; the lower fee data would decrease industry averages in the future as well as weaken the advisors' ability to charge fees at the high end of their schedule. Similarly, investors—particularly public pension sponsors—are reluctant to provide detailed data out of concern for being seen as having paid higher fees than were negotiated by industry peers.

Other Expenses

Indexing also lowers costs (other than advisory fees) that are incurred in investing assets including, for example, custodian and master trustee costs. Custodian costs vary in part as a function of the level of transaction activity in a portfolio. Since index funds have lower asset turnover and hence fewer transactions, the associated custodian costs also are lower.

Master trustee costs, too, vary in part as a function of the number of portfolios that are in trusteeship: fewer investment advisors and, hence, portfolios, result in lower master trustee costs. Since indexing often results in a consolidation of advisors responsible for managing a pool of assets, the associated master trustee costs are lower. The size of assets given to any single index fund advisor is generally much larger than the size of assets given to any single advisor for active management. In the summer of 1986, for example, the State Universities Retirement System of Illinois transferred fixed income assets from four active and passive investment advisors to a single index fund advisor. In the summer of 1987, the California State Teachers Retirement System transferred $6.3 billion of fixed income assets from at least eight investment advisors to a single index fund advisor.

In as much as indexing results in consolidation, it also reduces the time and resources required to supervise and coordinate a smaller number of investment advisors. A pension officer, for example, will have to spend less time reviewing fewer quarterly, semi-annual and annual performance reports, and less time attending fewer performance review meetings as a result of consolidation.

Similarly, indexing reduces the frequency, and therefore the associated costs, of searching for new investment advisors. Index fund advisors are less likely to be terminated because of poor performance, which results in a lower turnover of advisors. It should be noted that while lower turnover may be a direct benefit to investors, it is clearly disadvantageous to consultants who often are retained to assist in the search for new investment advisors. At least some consultants, therefore, might be expected to resist the move toward indexing.

Shift in Control

Another major advantage of indexing is the degree of control afforded the investor. When an investor hires an active investment advisor, the investor is largely at the mercy of the advisor. While an advisor is constrained by his investment discipline, there is, nevertheless, tremendous latitude afforded within that discipline. As such, the investor has minimal control over the advisor's investments at any point in time.

Indexing, on the other hand, allows the investor to specify both the benchmark as well as the degree of latitude allowed the index fund manager for deviation from the benchmark characteristics. For example, an active interest rate forecaster may have the latitude to construct a portfolio with any average duration that he deems appropriate whereas an index fund advisor may be limited to, say, a 10 percent deviation from the average duration of the index.

Indexing, therefore, allows investors the flexibility to choose a benchmark that meets their objectives and risk tolerance levels, and it provides the certainty that the benchmark characteristics will be closely tracked.

This particular advantage of indexing has become more important, following the issuance in December 1985 of two statements by the Financial Accounting Standards Board (commonly referred to as FASB 87). FASB 87 calls for new methods of accounting for defined benefit pension plans on corporate balance sheets and income statements. For example, if pension assets are not sufficient to cover the expected liabilities, the corporate balance sheet must reflect such relative underfunding by including a pension-related liability. Similarly, the income statement must reflect a pension expense that, through time, would reduce the shortfall in assets. While measuring the degree of shortfall and calculating the consequent expenses is complex and only accurate under certain assumptions, it is clear that FASB 87 has prompted many corporate pension plan sponsors to extend the duration of fixed income assets to match or approach the relatively long duration of pension liabilities. Many sponsors have done so by indexing a portion of their pension assets against long duration benchmarks such as the Salomon Brothers Large Pension Fund Baseline Bond Index.

Measuring Value Added

Finally, another advantage of indexing is the ease and precision with which the value added by the investment advisor can be measured. The performance of investment advisors is reviewed by investors and consultants on a quarterly basis. The review report includes the total return of the portfolio as well as the total return of a benchmark. To date, broad market indexes have been the most widely used benchmarks. The review process, however, has two shortcomings: the selected benchmarks often are not the appropriate performance bogey for the investment advisor; and the portfolio deviations from the benchmark characteristics which explain relative underperformance or outperformance are not thoroughly examined.

Indexing overcomes both shortcomings. First, establishing an index fund begins with an extensive search for the appropriate index, and therefore, the appropriate performance bogey. Second, index fund investors focus more closely on the quarterly differences in return between the portfolio and the benchmark, and require index fund advisors to attribute differences in return to specific deviations from the benchmark characteristics. For example, if an index fund outperforms the targeted index by 20 basis points, the outperformance must be attributed to, say, overweighting or underweighting one market sector relative to the index. Such detailed performance attribution, in turn, helps distinguish between random differences in return and actual value added by the investment advisor.

DISADVANTAGES

The rapid growth in its popularity notwithstanding, indexing does pose some disadvantages. These include relatively poor performance in periods of rising interest rates; the cost of foregone alternatives with higher expected returns; higher total return volatility, and, finally, inflexible investment requirements. Most of these disadvantages, however, can be overcome.

Bear Market Cycle Performance

In periods of rising interest rates which characterize bear bond market cycles, index funds tracking broad market benchmarks measure relatively poor or, at best, mediocre performance. Such poor performance has occurred over all recent bear market cycles.

Since the beginning of 1973,[3] interest rates have risen significantly during four periods as shown in Exhibit 1-6: January 1973 through September 1974; January 1977 through September 1981; April 1983 through June 1984; and, most recently, April 1987 through March 1989. In the latter three periods, the median active investment advisor outperformed market indexes and in the first period, the median active investment advisor matched the market index.

Exhibit 1-7 compares the annualized return of active investment advisors with those of the Lehman Brothers Aggregate and Government/Corporate Indexes for the last three bear market cycles. Similar data for a protracted bear market cycle including the January 1973–September 1974 and January 1977–September 1981 periods is also shown. For this protracted bear market cycle, the market index (Lehman Brothers Government/Corporate Index prior to 1976 and the Lehman Brothers Aggregate Index thereafter) matched

3. Data for Lehman Brothers indexes (the indexes with the longest historical data) start in January 1973.

Exhibit 1-6. Yield-to-Maturity of the Lehman Brothers Government/Corporate Index (1/31/73–12/31/89)

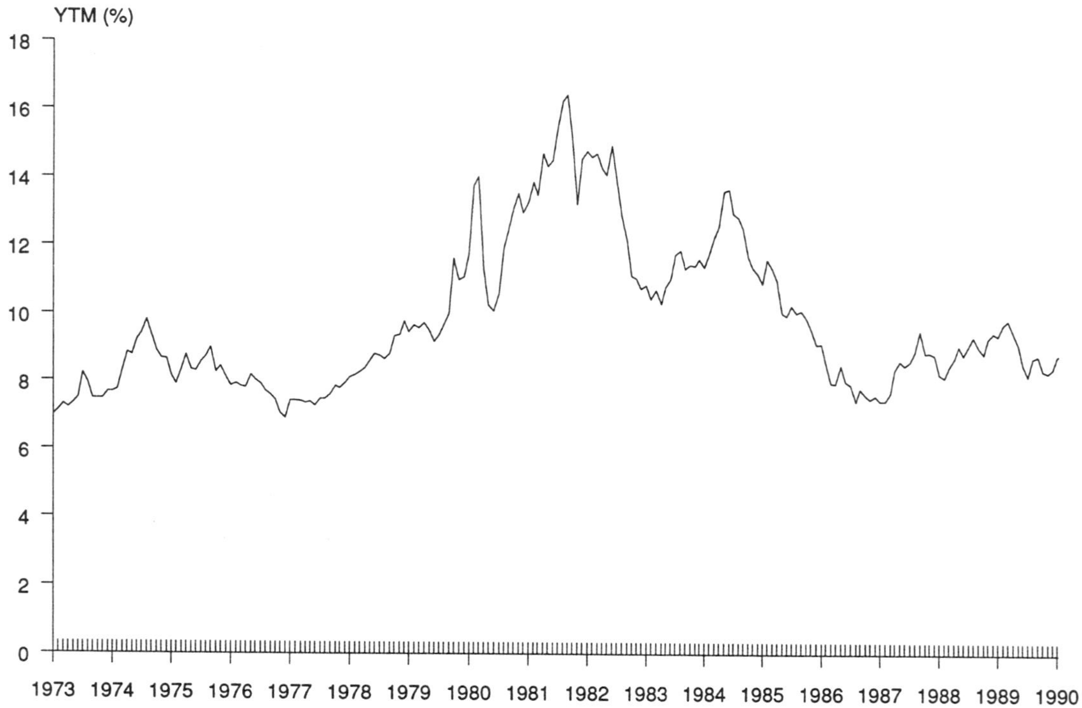

Exhibit 1-7. Annualized Total Return For Fixed Income Funds: Bear Market Cycles

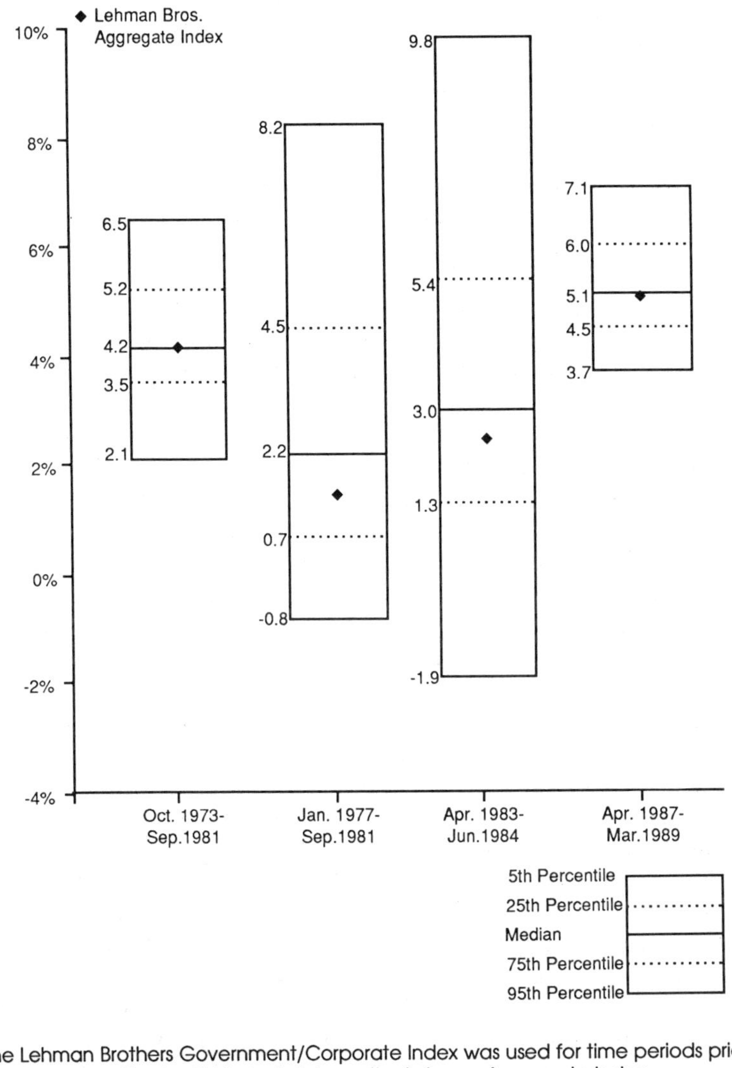

*The Lehman Brothers Government/Corporate Index was used for time periods prior to 1976 because of lack of historical data on the Lehman Aggregate Index.
Source: SEI Corporation.

the returns of the median active investment advisor. Between January 1977 and September 1981, which spans 57 months and an interest rate increase of 9.52 percentage points, the Lehman Brothers Government/Corporate Index measured an annualized return at 1.4 percent, equivalent to the return at the 60th percentile level of active investment advisors. Similarly, during the two recent bear market cycles, the Lehman Brothers Aggregate Index measured an annualized return below the median active investment advisor.

Thus, index funds tracking broad market benchmarks have underperformed active investment advisors in bear market cycles. The relative underperformance in periods of rising interest rates, however, has been offset by the relative outperformance of the benchmark in periods of falling interest rates (which characterizes a bull bond market cycle). Over complete market cycles, therefore, index funds tracking broad market benchmarks have, at best, outperformed and, at worst, matched the median active investment advisor.

As illustrated earlier in Exhibit 1-1 for the 10-year period ending December 1989 (which includes both bear and bull market cycles), the Salomon BIG Index ranked at the 19th percentile level, outperforming 81 percent of active investment advisors. Similarly for the eighth-year period ending in September 1981 (which includes a protracted bear market cycle), the Lehman Brothers Government/Corporate Index matched the median investment advisor as shown in Exhibit 1-7.

Of course, some investors will not tolerate the relative underperformance of a broad market benchmark during a protracted bear market cycle in anticipation of relative outperformance sometime in the future. In such cases, though, the problem is not the indexing strategy per se, but rather the inappropriateness of the benchmark. Broad market benchmarks, unlike active investment advisors, do not have a money market securities (securities with terms-to-maturity equal to or less than one year at issuance) component, and cannot eliminate their securities with long maturities; therefore, index funds have little protection against negative price returns in periods of rising rates. Investors, however, can select a benchmark with a shorter average duration and term-to-maturity than those of a broad market index; such a benchmark will have higher returns than broad market benchmarks in periods of rising interest rates. The Lehman Brothers Intermediate Government/Corporate Index is one such benchmark. For example, in the bear market cycle between January 1977 and September 1981, the Lehman Brothers Intermediate Government/Corporate Index measured an annualized return of 4.0 percent, which ranked well above the median and exceeded the Lehman Brothers Government/Corporate Index's annualized return of 1.4 percent.

Foregone Alternatives

While indexing may be more attractive than traditional active management based on interest rate anticipation, it entails a high opportunity cost (defined as the incremental returns foregone by not investing in market sectors with the highest performance). These market sectors include different maturity sectors as well as different types of securities such as Treasuries, agencies, corporates, Yankees, and mortgage-backed securities.

The cost of foregone alternatives is significant as shown in Exhibit 1-8. The performance of the Lehman Brothers Government/Corporate Index since 1973 is compared to that of the best performing market sector among the various Lehman Brothers subindexes and the three-month Treasury bill. The difference between the best performing market sector and the index represents the opportunity cost in absolute total returns. The opportunity cost also is expressed in relative terms as a percent of the returns of the best performing market sector.

The foregone returns in the last 17 years have averaged 48 percent of the returns of the highest performing market sector. In other words, the Lehman Brothers Government/Corporate Index has captured, on average, only 52 percent of the returns of the best performing market sector. The range of foregone returns over this period has been wide; in 1974, indexing against the Lehman Brothers Government/Corporate Index had a relative opportunity cost of

Exhibit 1-8. Opportunity Cost of Indexing

	Highest Performance Sector	*Return*	*Lehman Brothers Gov't./Corporate Index*	*Opportunity Cost Absolute*	*Opportunity Cost Relative*
	1	*2*	*3*	*4 = 2 − 3*	*5 = 4 / 2*
1973	T-Bills	6.76%	2.28%	4.48%	66.27%
1974	T-Bills	8.70%	0.17%	8.53%	98.05%
1975	Long Corporates	17.56%	12.29%	5.27%	30.01%
1976	Long Corporates	21.03%	15.59%	5.44%	25.87%
1977	Yankees	5.23%	2.98%	2.25%	43.02%
1978	T-Bills	6.97%	1.19%	5.78%	82.93%
1979	T-Bills	10.37%	2.30%	8.07%	77.82%
1980	T-Bills	12.28%	3.06%	9.22%	75.08%
1981	T-Bills	16.46%	7.26%	9.20%	55.89%
1982	Long Agencies	44.52%	31.09%	13.43%	30.17%
1983	Intermediate Corporates	10.66%	8.00%	2.66%	24.95%
1984	Long Corporates	17.66%	15.02%	2.64%	14.95%
1985	Long Treasuries	31.56%	21.30%	10.26%	32.51%
1986	Long Treasuries	24.10%	15.62%	8.48%	35.19%
1987	T-Bills	6.73%	2.29%	4.44%	65.97%
1988	Long Corporates	10.49%	7.58%	2.91%	27.74%
1989	Long Agencies	20.61%	14.24%	6.37%	30.91%
				Avg.	48.08%

Note: Returns for Treasury Bills since 1979 are from the Merrill Lynch 91-day Treasury Bill Index. Data prior to 1979 was estimated from DRI Inc. data.

98 percent; in 1984 the relative opportunity cost was only 15 percent.

Even though the Lehman Brothers Government/Corporate Index has captured only 52 percent of the returns of the best performing market sector, this percentage is still higher than the returns of active investment advisors. Therefore indexing only entails a significant opportunity cost if alternative strategies are available that capture consistently more than 52 percent of the returns of the best performing market sector. Several strategies have been developed over the last several years that have outperformed the Lehman Brothers Government/Corporate Index over a complete market cycle and have captured more than 52 percent of the returns of the best performing market sector based on simulated data.

Most of these strategies respond to, rather than forecast, changes in interest rates and changes in yield spreads between short-term securities and long-term securities. Examples of such strategies include (i) momentum-based strategies that use different short-term and long-term moving averages of bond prices to determine whether to invest in bonds or in short-term instruments; (ii) options-based strategies that use options theory to create, synthetically, a call option on the best performing market sector; and (iii) constant-duration and duration-averaging strategies that assume the mean-reversion of interest rates and maximize return by selling convexity over a complete market cycle of interest rates.

Some of these strategies have outperformed broad market benchmarks over bull, bear and, therefore, complete interest rate cycles. The same strategies, however, have underperformed during short periods characterized by volatile interest rates and by small overall changes in interest rate from the beginning to the end of the period. Other strategies have outperformed broad market benchmarks over complete interest cycles as well as during volatile interest rate environments. The long-term performance of these new and, therefore, untested strategies relative to indexing will depend on the market environment for interest rates and the actual implementation of the strategies with real assets.

Market Volatility

One of the disadvantages of index funds based on broad market benchmarks is their higher volatility of quarterly returns relative to the returns of active investment advisors.

Exhibit 1-9 compares the volatility of quarterly returns (defined as the annualized standard deviation of quarterly returns) of the Salomon BIG Index to the volatility of active investment advisors at the 5th, 25th, 50th (median), 75th, and 95th percentile level. In each of the five-year periods between 1978 and 1989, the Salomon BIG Index had a higher volatility of quarterly returns than the median active investment advisor. In some five-year periods such as the 1980–1984 period and the 1985–1989 period, the Salomon BIG Index measured a higher level of volatility than 67 percent of active investment advisors. The relatively greater level of volatility of returns also corresponds to a period of heightened volatility of interest rates, as shown in Exhibit 1-10.

Exhibit 1-10 is a graph of bond market volatility, measured by the standard deviation of price returns (derived from a yield series) for moving 12-month periods for a constant-maturity, 20-year Treasury security. As shown in the exhibit, volatility increased nearly five-fold between October 1979 and June 1980, (triggered by the Federal Reserve Board decision in October 1979 to stop using Federal Funds rate to implement monetary policy and instead focus on monetary and economic indicators).

Volatility of quarterly returns of the Salomon BIG Index is higher than the volatility of the median active investment advisor over longer periods as well. Exhibit 1-11 compares the volatility and the corresponding total return of the Salomon BIG Index to active investment advisors for the ten-year period ending December 1989. The horizontal axis measures the annualized volatility of quarterly returns; the vertical axis measures the annualized total return. Each observation marked by an asterisk represents the volatility and total return of one active fixed income investment advisor between 1980 and 1989. The horizontal and vertical lines that cross in the middle of the diagram represent median total return and median volatility, respectively. As shown in the exhibit, the Salomon BIG

Exhibit 1-9. Annualized Quarterly Volatility For Fixed Income Fund (For Moving 5-year Periods Ending December 31)

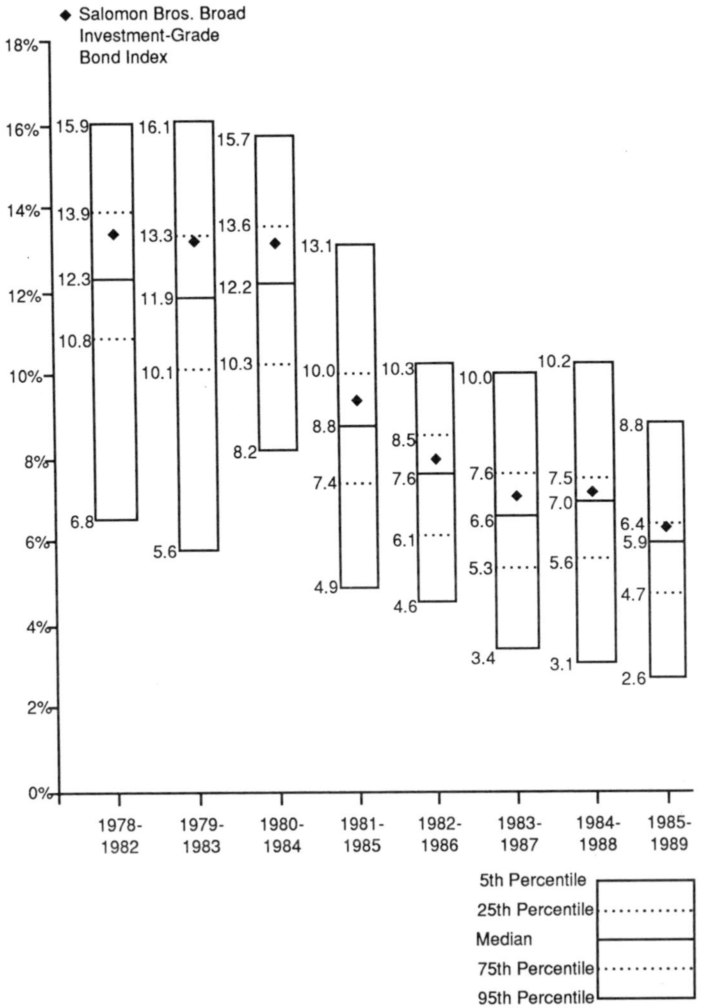

*The Lehman Brothers Aggregate Index was used for time periods prior to 1980 because of lack of data on Salomon Index.
Source: SEI Corporation.

Exhibit 1-10. Market Volatility (12-Month Yield Volatility for Constant Maturity 20-Year Treasury)

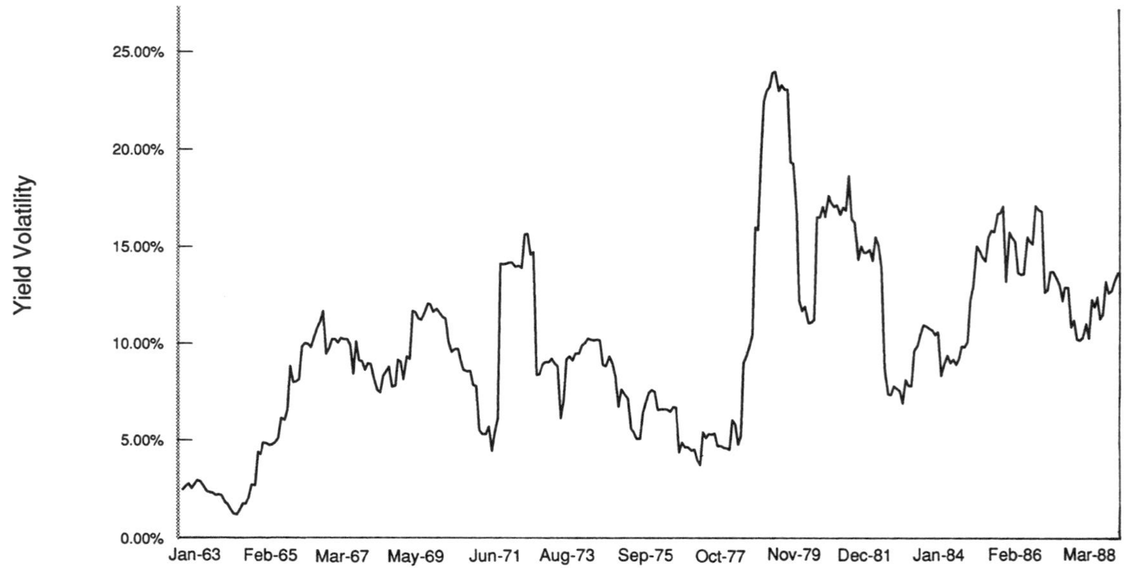

Source: Kidder, Peabody & Co. Inc.

Exhibit 1-11. Total Return Volatility: Market Benchmark Relative to Fixed Income Funds (For 10-Year Period Ending December 1989)

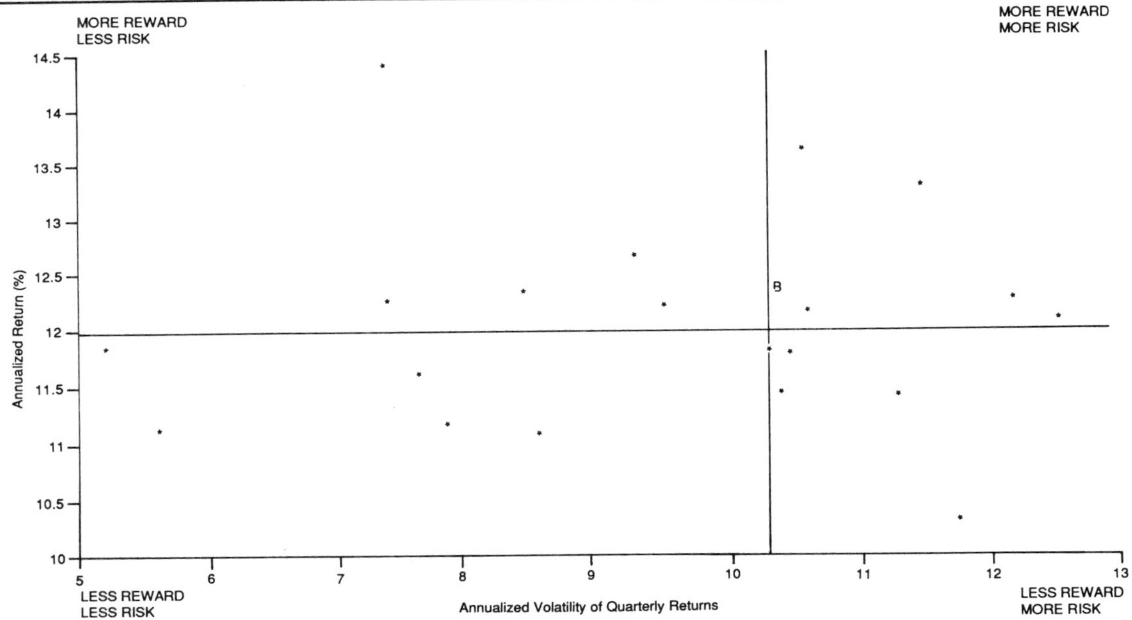

B = Salomon Brothers Broad Investment-Grade Bond Index
* Other Funds

Source: SEI Corporation.

Index represented by the letter "B" measured a higher volatility of quarterly returns than the median active investment advisor over this ten-year period.

Therefore, because index funds track broad market benchmarks, they will have higher total return volatility than the median active investment advisor. Investors who focus on volatility of quarterly returns or who are particularly concerned about heightened interest-rate volatility should use index funds based on benchmarks with shorter average duration and term-to-maturity than a broad market benchmark. Again, as mentioned earlier in discussing the bear market cycle performance of indexing, this disadvantage is attributable to the benchmark and not to the indexing strategy itself.

It is important to note some of the factors that have contributed to higher volatility of interest rates (see Exhibit 1-10)—and consequently higher volatility of quarterly returns for broad market benchmarks—in the last decade. These factors include: (i) financial deregulation, which has allowed for a diverse group of market participants, and also a diverse group of securities; (ii) technological innovation which has allowed for the rapid dissemination and analysis of information and has shortened the market participants' response time; (iii) change in profile of market participants (e.g. increased role of mutual funds and Japanese institutions), many of whom have different—if not shorter—investment horizons; and finally, (iv) increased complexity in designing securities such as derivatives that allow for easy and efficient transactions.

Rigid Requirements

Index funds also are criticized for their rigid requirements. "True" (also called "straight" or "vanilla") index funds do not invest in instruments outside the benchmark universe, thereby foregoing the opportunities and incremental return afforded by these instruments.

The broad market benchmarks exclude many sectors of the fixed income market. In the Treasury market, zero coupon Treasuries are excluded. In the mortgage-backed securities market, nonfederal agency conventional mortgage pass-throughs (e.g., those issued by Sears Mortgage Securities and Citibank), collateralized mortgage obligations, and interest-only and principal-only strips are excluded. In the corporate market, many asset-backed securities such as amortizing CARDS and CARS and medium-term notes are excluded. Derivative instruments such as futures contracts and options also are excluded. The potential uses of such instruments in index funds are described in Chapter 5.

Exhibit 1-12 lists six large sectors of the fixed income market that are excluded from broad market benchmarks. The estimated outstanding market value of each sector as of December 1989 also is shown. These sectors have been excluded by index producers for some combination of the following reasons: the underlying collat-

Exhibit 1-12. Investment-Grade, Fixed-Income Securities excluded from Broad Market Indexes

Sector	*Range of Estimated Market Value Outstanding (12/31/89) (in billions)*
Collateralized Mortgage Obligations	$226-280
Conventional (Private) Mortgage-Backed Securities	20-40
Mortgage-Backed Interest Only & Principal Only Strips	20
Asset-Backed Securities	40-50
Medium-Term Notes	80-100
Treasury STRIPS	83-96

Source: Based on data from Lehman Brothers Inc., Bear Stearns, Goldman Sachs Mortgage Securities Research, Merrill Lynch Capital Markets, and First Boston Corporation.

eral of the instrument is included in the index; the securities are not registered with the Securities and Exchange Commission; the market value of the sector is too small to have any impact on the index; or reliable data is not available.

While true index funds are constrained by the holdings of their benchmarks, this constraint can be overcome readily by enhanced index funds. Enhanced index funds, which are described in Chapter 5, have the flexibility to invest in securities outside their index universe, benefitting from the incremental return from such securities and circumventing the rigid requirements posed by true index funds.

Chapter 2

Selecting the Index

Selecting the appropriate index is the single most important decision when indexing a fixed income portfolio, overwhelming the impact of other decisions such as choice of an enhanced or straight index fund, selection of an index fund manager, and the degree of latitude allowed the fund manager. For, importantly, the index defines the portfolio's key characteristics. These characteristics include: maturity and duration structures which, in turn, determine the portfolio's return in response to changes in both interest rates and the shape of the yield curve; exposure to different market sectors such as Treasury, corporate and mortgage-backed securities; and the average credit quality and minimum credit rating required for any security included in the index fund.

Several factors should be considered prior to selecting an index to ensure that an investor's particular requirements are met. Investors often have differing objectives, risk tolerance levels, investment horizons, and regulatory concerns that govern whether and how to use fixed income securities.

Some investors use bonds with the objective of minimizing total return volatility, others to generate a stream of cash flows, and still others as a hedge against deflation. If minimizing total return volatility is the primary objective, investors will seek a short- or intermediate-duration index. If bonds are used to meet particular liability payments, investors will seek an index with securities that generate the necessary cash flows. And if protection against deflation is a major objective, investors will require a longer-duration index.

Similarly, differing levels of risk tolerance determine the type of index selected. Investors who are wary of risking the principal value of their assets will want a short-duration index containing securities with high credit quality. Investors who are concerned about the performance of their assets relative to a universe of active investment advisors will choose traditional market indexes with returns that have at times exceeded the performance of as many as three-quarters of all investment advisors.

Investment horizons bear on the choice of an index as well. A short investment horizon may discourage investors from selecting an index with high quality corporate and mortgage-backed securities; the benefit of the incremental yield of corporate and mortgage-backed securities relative to Treasury securities is small if the securities are held for a short period. Furthermore, there is a high risk of losing this small benefit if the yield spread between corporate and mortgage-backed securities relative to Treasury securities widens. Conversely, a long investment horizon will lead to selecting a diversified index that includes all sectors of the bond market; the incremental yield obtained by investing in corporate and mortgage-backed securities can be significant when the yield is compounded over a long horizon.

Finally, regulatory constraints, where they exist, also guide the choice of an index. Among such regulatory constraints are maturity constraints which prohibit investment in securities beyond certain maturities, and sector constraints which prohibit investment in securities that are not guaranteed by the full faith and credit of the U.S. Government.

ALTERNATIVE INDEXES

Fixed income portfolio indexes fall into four categories: broad market indexes; broad market sub-indexes; specialized market sector indexes; and customized indexes. Broad market indexes are those designed to be representative of the mainstream of the fixed income securities market. Broad market sub-indexes partition the mainstream fixed income market by sector, maturity, quality, and coupon, among others. Specialized market sector indexes represent fixed income securities outside the mainstream, notably zero-coupon and high-yield indexes. And finally, customized indexes are tailor-made to meet those requirements and objectives of an investor that cannot be satisfied with the generic indexes.

Typically, these indexes measure the total return of a universe of securities. Total return consists of four components: price return from changes in the market value of the securities; income return from coupon payment and changes in level of accrued interest; reinvestment return from reinvestment of cash flows received; and for mortgage-backed securities, principal return from decreases in the amount outstanding of the securities (including amortization and prepayment of principal).

In most indexes, each individual security is weighted either by its outstanding market value or by its outstanding par value. Both market value and par value weightings are designed to give large issues a greater role in the total return of an index. Such weighting in the fixed income market is, in fact, a vestige of capital market theory which suggests that in the equity market, individual stocks in an efficient portfolio should be weighted by their capitalization.

There are some indexes, notably in the specialized market sector category, in which all securities receive equal weighting. The advantages of equal par value weighting of securities are two-fold: accuracy of calculation and better reflection of how securities are purchased for a given portfolio.

An equal-weighted average of all securities in an index is a much simpler and, thus, often a more accurate calculation. In the Treasury market, market value or par value weightings can be problematic; Treasury securities have been stripped into zero coupon securities since 1981, thereby reducing the par value of the amount outstanding of stripped Treasury securities. Most Treasury indexes, however, have not adjusted downward the remaining par value outstanding of stripped Treasury securities. Similarly, mortgage-backed securities indexes do not adjust downward the principal amount outstanding of mortgage-backed securities by the principal amount used as collateral for Collateralized Mortgage Obligations.

The second advantage of equal weighting of securities in indexes is that this method better reflects how investment advisors buy securities for a portfolio. Investment advisors do not buy securities in the same proportion as the market value or par value outstanding of each security; rather, each security is purchased on the basis of its expected risk and return profile and its expected contribution to the risk and return profile of the entire portfolio. Par value outstanding becomes important only inasmuch as large par values imply greater liquidity of securities in the secondary market, and small par values imply lesser liquidity.

Data on most indexes is produced on a monthly basis. The data includes total, price, and income returns as well as average index characteristics such as maturity, coupon, yield, nominal duration, and effective or option-adjusted duration. Data on some indexes is produced on a daily basis, partly due to the increased interest in indexing and partly due to a greater emphasis on short-term performance. It is important to note that, for some indexes, daily data requires pricing thousands of securities.

Individual securities are priced either by market traders who are active in bidding for and offering securities throughout the day, or by means of a system sometimes referred to as matrix-pricing. In matrix-pricing, a computer-driven model prices securities relative to a core of securities that have been priced by traders. In some indexes, all securities included are priced directly by traders; other indexes are based on a combination of trader- and matrix-pricing.

Broad Market Indexes

The three predominant, true broad market indexes are the Salomon Brothers Broad Investment-Grade Bond Index (Salomon BIG Index), the Lehman Brothers Aggregate Index (Lehman Aggregate Index) and the Merrill Lynch Domestic Master Index (Merrill Domestic Master). All three indexes are market-value weighted, total return indexes The Salomon BIG Index is a monthly index and the two latter are daily indexes.

Designed to be representative of the mainstream of the fixed income securities market, these broad bond market indexes cover the government, corporate, mortgage-backed, and Yankee sectors.

The government sector includes publicly-traded securities issued by the U.S. Treasury, as well as other government agencies and quasi-federal entities. Government securities comprise the single largest sector of the fixed income market, accounting for 50 to 60 percent of the broad indexes. (See Exhibit 2-1.) Government securities also represent the most liquid sector of the fixed income market due to their large volume outstanding ($1.5 trillion) and overall credit quality.

The corporate sector covers publicly-traded, fixed-rate, nonconvertible corporate securities that are registered with the Securities and Exchange Commission (SEC) and have a minimum credit rating of Baa3 by Moody's Investor Service or BBB- by Standard and Poor's Corporation. Issues below these rating levels are considered

Exhibit 2-1. Fixed Income Market by Sectors

(as of 12/31/89, $ billions)

Treasuries	$1,245.5	46.5%
Agencies (govt. sponsored)	219.2	8.2%
Corporates	428.8	16.0%
Yankees	56.5	2.1%
GNMAs	325.1	12.1%
FHLMCs	190.4	7.1%
FNMAs	137.0	5.1%
FHA/GNMA Project Loans	6.4	0.2%
15-Year MBS	72.4	2.7%
Total	$2,681.3	100.0%

Source: Salomon Brothers Inc., Merrill Lynch Capital Markets and Lehman Brothers Inc.; numbers are based on data on the three broad indexes.

below investment-grade and are only included in high yield indexes. The corporate sector accounts for about 16 percent of the broad indexes. Corporate securities that are issued and distributed through a private placement are excluded from the broad market indexes.

The mortgage-backed sector includes fixed-rate mortgage pass-through securities issued by the Government National Mortgage Association (GNMA or Ginnie Mae), the Federal Home Loan Mortgage Corporation (FHLMC or Freddie Mac), and the Federal National Mortgage Association (FNMA or Fannie Mae). The mortgage-backed sector accounts for about 27 percent of the broad indexes, with GNMAs representing 12 percent, FHLMCs seven percent, and FNMAs five percent. The distinctions among the three types of mortgage-backed securities are outlined in Appendix B. Fifteen-year mortgage-backed securities account for an additional three percent. Adjustable rate mortgage-backed securities (ARMs) and private or conventional mortgage-backed securities are excluded from the indexes. (Private or conventional mortgage-backed securities are issued by corporate entities such as grantor trusts, mortgage corporations, savings and loans association, and commercial banks.)

The fourth sector in the broad indexes is the Yankee bond sector. This sector covers U.S. dollar-denominated, SEC-registered, publicly-traded, fixed-rate, non-convertible debt issued by international (or supranational) organizations, foreign government entities including national (or "sovereign") and provincial (or "local") governments, and other official agencies. Debt issued by Canadian corporations that meet the above criteria also are included in the Yankee bond sector.

Among international organizations, the World Bank, formally known as the International Bank for Reconstruction and Development, is the single largest issuer of Yankee bonds. At year-end 1989, the market value of securities issued by the World Bank was about $7.7 billion. All bonds issued by international organizations that are in the Salomon BIG Index are part of the government component of the Index.

Among foreign government and corporate issuers, Canadians comprise the largest group with a year-end 1989 market value of

$31.7 billion. Examples of Canadian issuers include the Province of Ontario, the Province of Nova Scotia, and Hydro-Quebec. Other large sovereign issuers are the Kingdom of Sweden and the Commonwealth of Australia. Yankee securities account for about two percent of the indexes. In the Lehman Aggregate Index, Yankee bonds were treated as a separate sector much like government, corporate and mortgage-backed securities sectors through the end of 1989; thereafter, Yankee bonds were incorporated into the corporate sector. In the Salomon BIG Index and the Merrill Domestic Master, Yankee securities are part of the corporate sector.

All government, corporate, and Yankee notes and bonds that are included in the indexes must have a minimum remaining term-to-maturity of one year. As securities shorten in maturity and fall below the one-year minimum, they are removed from the indexes.

Inclusion by the three broad indexes of many of the same securities has resulted in similar cumulative returns. Between January 1980 (inception date for the Salomon BIG Index and, therefore, the earliest date for which historical returns are available) and December 1989, the Salomon BIG Index measured a total return of 221.2 percent (12.38 percent annualized), the Lehman Aggregate Index measured a total return of 222.7 percent (12.43 percent annualized and the Merrill Domestic Master measured a total return of 218.1 percent (12.27 percent annualized). The difference between the highest return (that of the Lehman Aggregate Index) and the lowest return (that of the Merrill Domestic Master) is very small: 16 basis points on an annualized basis. A basis point is one one-hundredth of one percent or 0.01 percent. The cumulative returns for each index are graphed in Exhibit 2-2.

While the difference in the annualized cumulative returns of the three broad market indexes is small, the difference in returns over shorter periods is larger. In 1982 for example, the Lehman Aggregate Index measured a return of 32.62 percent while Merrill Domestic Master measured a return of 30.91 percent—a difference of 171 basis points. It should be noted that 1982 was an exceptional year given high total annual returns as well as large differences in returns among the broad indexes. In other years the difference between the highest returning index and the lowest returning index

Exhibit 2.2 Cumulative Total Return for Broad Market Indexes

(1980-1989)

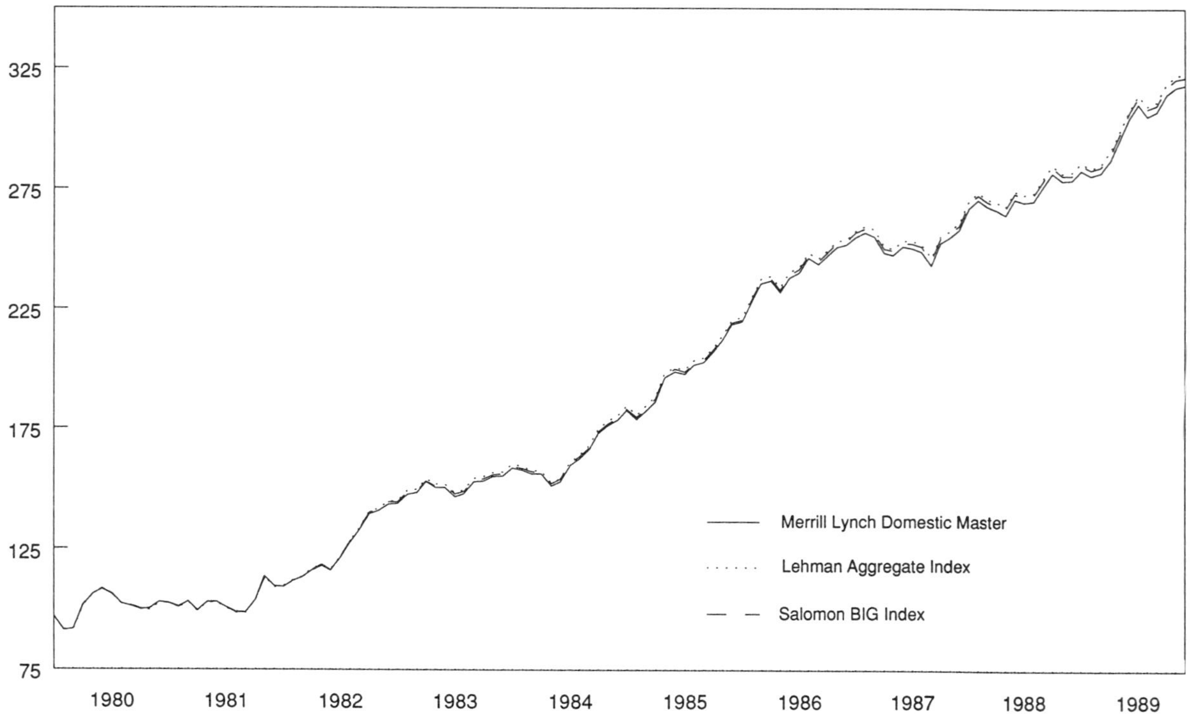

has averaged 27 basis points. Exhibit 2-3 provides the annual return for each of the three broad indexes; the last column measures the difference in the returns of the two indexes with the highest or lowest returns. Of the three indexes, the Lehman Aggregate Index and the Merrill Domestic Master have measured the highest return or lowest return most frequently, while the Salomon BIG Index primarily has measured returns that fall between those of the other two indexes. This consistency in the Salomon BIG Index may be attributed to the fact that all the securities in that index are priced by traders; such pricing may reduce year-end pricing biases and errors which usually are offset in subsequent years.

The differences in returns in the three indexes can be attributed to three factors: pricing, structure, and technical assumptions. Bonds in the indexes are not priced uniformly. In the fixed income market, unlike the equity market, most trading activity takes place in an over-the-counter (OTC) market rather than on an exchange. In the absence of a centralized exchange from which reliable closing prices

Exhibit 2-3. Annual Return For the Broad indexes

(in percent)

	Salomon BIG Index	*Lehman Aggregate Index*	*Merrill Domestic Master*	*Difference Between Highest and Lowest*
1980	2.82%	2.70% L	2.99% H	0.29%
1981	6.48% H	6.25% L	6.43%	0.23%
1982	31.78%	32.62% H	30.91% L	1.71%
1983	8.21%	8.35% H	8.03% L	0.32%
1984	14.98% L	15.15%	15.20% H	0.22%
1985	22.26%	22.10% L	22.40% H	0.30%
1986	15.45% H	15.26%	15.22% L	0.23%
1987	2.60%	2.76% H	2.40% L	0.36%
1988	7.98%	7.89% L	8.04% H	0.15%
1989	14.44%	14.53% H	14.18% L	0.35%

for the day can be obtained, traders from Salomon Brothers Inc., Lehman Brothers Inc., and Merrill Lynch Capital Markets may price the same bond at different levels. Such pricing discrepancies are more common in corporate and Yankee bonds and less so in Treasury, agency and mortgage-backed securities. In fact, in the corporate market, prices of less liquid issues (issues that do not trade frequently and have under $25 million par amount outstanding) can vary by as much as five percent.

The bonds in the indexes also are priced at different times of the day. In the Salomon BIG Index, bonds are priced at "the close of business," say, between 5:00 p.m. and 6:00 p.m. Eastern Standard Time or EST; in the Lehman Aggregate Index, at 3:00 p.m. EST; and in the Merrill Domestic Master, between 2:30 p.m. and 3:00 p.m. EST.

Finally, not all bonds in the indexes are priced by traders. The Salomon BIG Index is the only index in which all securities are priced by traders. In the Lehman Aggregate Index and the Merrill Domestic Master, most issues are priced by traders; but a small remainder—usually less than ten percent of the market value of the index—is priced by means of matrix-pricing.

While the structures of the three broad market indexes are largely similar, several key differences should be pointed out. The indexes differ with respect to the minimum amounts outstanding per issue required for inclusion in the index. The Salomon BIG Index only includes government and corporate securities that have at least $50 million outstanding at time of issuance and mortgage-backed securities that have at least $200 million outstanding. Securities that fall below the minimum with time due to sinking fund, defeasance, or prepayment are held in the index until they fall below $25 million outstanding. The Lehman Aggregate Index has a minimum requirement of $25 million outstanding for corporate and mortgage-backed securities and $100 million outstanding for government securities. The Merrill Domestic Master has a minimum requirement of $25 million outstanding for government and corporate securities, while the minimum requirement for mortgage-backed securities is $200 million outstanding. The minimum requirement for mortgage-backed securities in the three indexes is specified in terms of type and coupon of mortgage-backed security issued by any one agency (e.g., all Single-Family 8.5 percent coupon pools issued by GNMA, when aggregated, should meet the minimum requirement).

The indexes also differ in their inclusion or exclusion of several small sectors of the bond market. Exhibit 2-4 lists sectors that are included in at least one, but not all three, of the three broad market indexes. For example, the Salomon BIG Index includes Federal Housing Authority (FHA) and GNMA 223 (f) project loans. (See Appendix B for a description of project loans.) With a market value of about $6.4 billion at the end of 1989, these two sectors represent 0.2 percent of the market value of the Salomon BIG Index. Yet project loans are excluded from both the Lehman Aggregate Index and the Merrill Domestic Master.

The Lehman Aggregate Index and the Merrill Domestic Master, on the other hand, included GNMA II and Mobile Home mortgage-backed securities (Appendix B) through the end of 1989, neither of which were ever included in the Salomon BIG Index. At the end of 1989, the two sectors represented about one percent of the Lehman Aggregate Index and less than one percent of the Merrill Domestic Master since not as many issues and coupons meet Merrill Domestic Master's minimum outstanding selection criteria.

Exhibit 2-4. Sector Differences in the Broad Indexes

(as of 12/31/89, billions)[a]

Sector Name	*Title XI*	*GNMA II*	*Mobile Homes*	*Multi-Family Project Loan*
Market Value	$1.4	$19.5	$1.4	$6.4
Salomon BIG Index	Included	Excluded	Excluded	Included
Lehman Aggregate Index	Included[b]	Included[b]	Included	Excluded
Merrill Domestic Master	Excluded	Included[b]	Included[b]	Excluded

[a]Based on largest representation in any of the indexes as of 12/31/89.
[b]Sectors were dropped from indexes in 1990.

Title XI bonds (Appendix B) represent another sector that is not included in all three indexes. At a market value of about $1.4 billion at the end of 1989, this sector accounts for less than one-tenth of one percent of the Salomon BIG Index. In the Lehman Aggregate Index, Title XI bonds had a market value of $1.7 billion, or 0.07 percent of the index; these securities were removed from the Lehman Aggregate Index at year-end 1989. This sector is excluded from the Merrill Domestic Master.

Finally, bank deposit notes and certificates of deposit notes (Appendix B) are excluded from the Salomon BIG Index and the Lehman Aggregate Index. Those deposit notes (not issued through a continuous offering program) are included in the Merrill Domestic Master. The total market value outstanding for this sector is estimated at $10 billion.

The reasons cited for the exclusion of any specific sector from an index are small market value outstanding, limited availability and the consequent inaccurate pricing in the secondary market, and absence of reliable historical data. Deposit notes are excluded because of their irregular forms of issuance and their similarities to term certificates of deposit and commercial paper.

It should be noted that as sectors which are excluded from a particular index grow in size and importance in the bond market, they may be added to that index in the future. For example, the addition of all Yankee bonds to the Salomon BIG Index in January 1988 reflected the growing role of the Yankee sector in fixed income portfolios. Prior to January 1988, the Salomon BIG Index included only World Bank and Canadian bonds among the Yankee securities. As mentioned earlier in the chapter, at year-end in 1989, Yankee bonds represented about two percent of the broad market indexes.

In addition to small structural differences, the three indexes also differ in the technical assumptions made about reinvestment, timing of cash flows, accrued interest, and prepayment of mortgage-backed securities. In the Salomon BIG Index, all cash flows from government and corporate bonds received during the month are reinvested at the daily average 1-month Treasury bill rate for that month. In the Lehman Aggregate Index, the same cash flows are held at face value until the end of the month when they are reinvested in the Index portfolio. In the Merrill Domestic Master, cash flows from government and corporate bonds are reinvested in the government and corporate component of the Merrill Domestic Master when received.

Cash flows from mortgage-backed securities are treated differently; in all three indexes, the principal and interest payments received with a 45-day to 75-day delay are discounted back to the end of the previous month for that month's total return calculations. The Salomon BIG Index uses the average rate of the 1-month Treasury bill as a discount factor. The Lehman Aggregate Index uses the average rate of the current 3-month Treasury bill as a discount factor. Finally, the Merrill Domestic Master uses the yield on similar type current-coupon mortgage-backed securities as a discount factor.

The three indexes treat accrued interest for mortgage-backed securities differently as well. The Salomon BIG Index assumes an accrued interest of zero for calculating total return. The Lehman Aggregate Index uses the actual accrued interest for each mortgage-backed security on its appropriate settlement date and takes the present value of that accrued interest at the beginning of the month. And, the Merrill Domestic Master assumes an accrued interest of zero.

Finally, the three indexes use different prepayment levels to compute the yield-to-maturity, the effective yield, the Macaulay duration and the effective duration of mortgage-backed securities. The Salomon BIG Index uses Salomon Brothers Inc.'s long-term projected prepayment rate in an unchanged interest rate environment, the Lehman Aggregate Index uses the prepayment rate projected by the Public Securities Association (PSA) and the Merrill Domestic Master uses the Merrill Lynch Capital Markets' projected prepayment rate. The three different prepayment rates can result in very different yield and duration numbers particularly in a period of rapidly rising or falling prepayment levels. Historically, the differences in the yield and duration data were significant since the Lehman Aggregate Index used the historical prepayment rate for the last three months and the Merrill Domestic Master used the historical prepayment rate for the last 12 months. For example, in September 1986 after a period of rising prepayment levels, the duration of the mortgage-backed securities component of the Salomon BIG Index stood at 3.71 years. The duration of the Lehman Aggregate Index's mortgage-backed securities component was lower at 3.52 years, reflecting the higher, three-month historical prepayment rate used by Lehman Brothers Inc. The duration of the Merrill Domestic Master mortgage-backed securities component was the highest, at 5.04 years. The historical prepayment rate for the last 12 months used by Merrill Lynch Capital Markets was much lower than both Salomon Brothers Inc.'s long-term projected prepayment rate and Lehman Brothers Inc.'s three-month prepayment rate.

The approach to calculating the maturity for mortgage-backed securities also is different in the three indexes. In the Salomon BIG Index, the projected long-term prepayment rate is used for a weighted average life. In the Lehman Aggregate Index, the PSA projected prepayment rate is used. However, in the Merrill Domestic Master, the final maturity date is based on a non-prepaying amortization schedule. The different approaches result in different average maturities for the three indexes. As shown in Exhibit 2-5, the average maturity for Merrill Domestic Master is much longer than the other two indexes, primarily because of the different computation methodology for the maturity (weighted average life) of the mortgage-backed securities component.

Apart from the impact on the indexes' average maturity, the differences in structure and technical assumptions have little impact on the average characteristics of the three indexes. As shown in Exhibit 2-5, the three indexes have similar market values (between $2.6 trillion and $2.7 trillion) and have similar average coupons, yields and nominal durations.

The differences in effective (also referred to as option-adjusted) durations of the three indexes is explained by the different models used to calculate the call exposure of the corporate bonds and prepayment exposure of the mortgage-backed securities. Each firm has developed a proprietary option model and prepayment model, and uses a different interest-rate volatility assumption to adjust for the uncertainty of cash flows of corporate bonds and mortgage-backed securities.

Exhibit 2-5. Profile of Bond Indexes
(as of 12/31/89)

	Salomon BIG Index	*Lehman Aggregate Index*	*Merrill Domestic Master*
Market Value (billions)	$2,580.6	$2,684.6	$2,702.7
Number of Issues	4871	6145	4776
Coupon (percent)	9.01%	9.26%	9.32%
Yield (percent)	8.67%	8.66%	8.65%
Maturity (years)	9.53	9.92	13.6
Macaulay Duration (years)	5.25	5.35	5.08
Effective (Option-Adjusted) Duration (years)	4.56	4.75	NA

Many investors have selected a broad market index for indexing their fixed income assets, including some of the largest U.S. corporate and public pension plans. Several mutual funds also have been set up to provide returns that match the broad market indexes.

Typically, investors have chosen a broad index for three reasons: relative returns, exposure to all key sectors of the fixed income market, and the precepts of capital market theory. Historically, the returns of broad indexes have been higher than median fixed income investment advisors as measured by various performance evaluation services. In effect, investors who have chosen a broad index have selected the past relative performance of the broad market indexes. The broad indexes also provide exposure to the large and significant sectors of the fixed income market. In this case, investors have selected broad indexes as an efficient and low-cost means of investing across different sectors of the market. Broad market indexes have been selected also by investors who have extended capital market theory from the equity market to the fixed income market; as noted earlier, capital market theory argues that market capitalization-weighted equity portfolios represent an efficient approach to investment in the equity market. Such an extension was made despite the different roles that stocks and bonds play in any portfolio.

Components of Broad Indexes

Each of the broad market indexes can be broken down into multiple components or sub-indexes, based on market sector, maturity, quality, coupon, and industry. The most common breakdowns are by sector and by maturity. The broad indexes are broken down into Treasury, Agency, Corporate and Mortgage-Backed Securities sub-indexes. The Treasury, Agency, and Corporate components are broken down further by maturity into intermediate and long-term sub-indexes, where intermediate is defined as one- to 10-year maturities and long-term is defined as any maturity longer than 10 years. Mortgage-backed securities, on the other hand, are broken down first by agency into GNMA, FNMA, FHLMC, and where applicable, multi-family project loans; and second by original term-to-maturity into 30- year and 15-year mortgage-backed securities.

The number of sub-indexes published on a monthly basis varies from dealer to dealer. Salomon Brothers Inc. publishes data on nearly 140 sub-indexes in two monthly index reports ("Salomon Brothers Total Rate-of-Return Indexes" and "Mortgage Pass-Through Security Total Rate-of-Return Index"). Lehman Brothers Inc. publishes data on approximately 60 sub-indexes in a monthly index report ("The Bond Market Report"). Both dealers supplement published reports with additional data and further breakdowns or sub-indexes on request. Lehman Brothers Inc. data is available through an on-line system. Merrill Lynch Capital Markets publishes data on approximately 150 sub-indexes of the Merrill Domestic Master in a monthly report ("Taxable Bond Indexes"). In addition, daily total returns on some 860 Merrill Lynch Capital Markets indexes are available on "The Bloomberg."[1]

Some representative sub-indexes from the three broad indexes are listed in Exhibit 2-6. Of course, these sub-indexes represent only

1. "The Bloomberg" is an on-line fixed income and equity information system containing databases as well as software to analyze the data.

Exhibit 2-6. Example of Sub-Indexes Published in Monthly Reports

Salomon BIG Index

Treasury/GNMA: U.S. Treasuries and GNMA mortgage-backed securities, i.e., full faith and credit of U.S. Government.
Corporate 3-7: All corporates with maturities greater than or equal to 3 years and less than 7 years.
High-Grade Corporate: AAA-AA corporate bonds with maturities greater than ten years.
Multifamily Projects: 7.43% FHA Project Loans and GNMA 223(f) Project Loans.
Seasoned GNMA 8s: GNMAs with 8% coupons and five years of seasoning.

Lehman Aggregate Index

Government Bonds: All U.S. Treasury and Agency bonds.
Agency Intermediate: U.S. Agency bonds with maturities between one and ten years.
Industrial Intermediate: Industrial corporate bonds with maturities between one and ten years.
Sovereigns Long-Term: Foreign sovereign government debt with maturities of ten years or longer.
GNMA GPMs: GNMA Graduated Payment Mortgage-Backed Securities.

Merrill Domestic Master

Treasuries 3-4.99: All Treasuries with maturities between 3 and 4.99 years.
Long-Term Medium Quality: All corporate with A-BBB rating with maturities greater than 15 years.
Utilities Exc. Telephone High Quality: All utilities with AAA-AA rating excluding Telephones.
Yankees 5-9.99: All Yankee bonds with maturities between 5 and 9.99 years.
GNMA II SF 15 years: GNMA II Single Family mortgage-backed securities with original term of 15 years (not published after 12/31/89).

a handful of the components of each index. Each of the three indexes can be broken down into as many components as there are securities.

Many of the sub-indexes have been in existence longer than their broader counterparts. The Salomon Brothers Long-Term High-Grade Corporate Bond Index is among the earliest total return indexes. While it is currently a component of the Salomon BIG Index, the sub-index was introduced in 1973. It includes AAA and AA corporate bonds with a minimum maturity of ten years and shares the same market value selection criteria as the corporate bonds in the Salomon BIG Index (all the selection criteria for the Long-Term High-Grade Corporate Bond Index were redefined when the Salomon BIG Index was introduced).

Another sub-index which preceded its broader counterpart is the Lehman Brothers Government/Corporate Index. This index was introduced in 1979 and differs from the Lehman Aggregate Index in its exclusion of mortgage-backed securities and Yankee bonds.

There are two additional indexes designed to track sectors of the mainstream fixed income market: the Morgan Stanley Actively Traded MBS Index (Morgan Stanley MBS Index) and the Ryan Labs Treasury Index. While these indexes are not components or sub-indexes of any specific broad index, both track sectors that are included in the three key broad market indexes. The Morgan Stanley MBS Index is a monthly market-value weighted, trader-priced, total return index measuring the returns of the GNMA, FNMA, and FHLMC market. The distinguishing feature of this index is the extent of detailed information published on it. The data includes returns on all actively-traded (i.e., currently defined as full- and half-coupons below 13.50 percent coupon) sectors and coupon levels of the agency mortgage-backed securities market. Total return is broken down into income return, principal return, price return resulting from changes in interest rates and price return resulting from changes in option-adjusted spreads. The data also includes a distinction between seasoned and new issues (this distinction also is made in the mortgage-backed securities component of the Salomon BIG Index and that of the Merrill Domestic Master).

The second index is the Ryan Labs Treasury Index, which is a daily, equal- weighted, trader-priced total return index comprised of most recently auctioned 2-, 3-, 4-, 5-, 7-, 10-, and 30-year Treasuries.

The Lehman Brothers Government/Corporate Index was the most widely used benchmark for indexing through most of the 1980's, partly due to its availability in the early 1980's when indexing was in its infancy and mortgage-backed securities were a smaller sector of the bond market, and partly because many sponsors prefer to index government and corporate bond holdings and retain specialty managers to invest the mortgage-backed securities holdings. By year-end 1989, however, about 70 percent of the largest index funds were based on components of the Salomon BIG Index (see Appendix A).

Many investors also index assets against the government component of the broad indexes. This sub-index is selected as a conservative index since it reduces credit risk by excluding corporate and Yankee bonds. Others have chosen the government component to accommodate regulatory requirements that prevent them from investing in corporate bonds. And finally, some have chosen the government component since they believe that the extra yield from corporate bonds does not adequately compensate investors for the additional credit risk and the risk associated with callable corporate bonds.

Specialized Indexes

A third group of indexes are those designed to track a specialized sector outside the mainstream of the fixed income market. In the government bond market, for example, there are indexes for zero-coupon Treasuries that have been stripped from intermediate and long-term Treasuries. Among them are the Merrill Lynch STRIPS and TIGR Indexes, which track various maturities of zero coupon Treasuries issued by Merrill Lynch Capital Markets and are known as Treasury Investment Growth Receipts. Salomon Brothers Inc. tracks the zero-coupon Treasury market through its STRIPS (Separate Trading of Registered Interest and Principal Securities) Indexes.

The Salomon Indexes differentiate between the interest component and the principal or corpus component of each STRIPS.

In the corporate sector, several indexes have been introduced since 1983 to track high-yield (or junk) and convertible bonds. The high-yield market is tracked by the Donaldson Lufkin & Jenrette High Yield Index, the First Boston High Yield Index, the Salomon Brothers Composite High-Yield Index and the Merrill Lynch High Yield Master. Unlike the broad market indexes which have similar designs, the high-yield indexes are very different in several important respects. Notably, the selection criteria are not as objective across the indexes. In the Donaldson Lufkin & Jenrette High Yield Index and the Lehman Brothers High Yield Index, assessment of liquidity and availability determine whether or not an issue is included in the Indexes. The First Boston Corporation, Salomon Brothers Inc. and Merrill Lynch Capital Markets, on the other hand, use well-defined criteria for including or excluding securities in their indexes but those criteria differ. The criteria are summarized in Exhibit 2-7.

The convertible bond market is tracked by several indexes as well, notably First Boston Convertible Securities Index, the Goldman Sachs Convertible 100, the Merrill Lynch Convertible Master Index, and the Froley Revy Convertible Bond Index. The First Boston Convertible Securities Index is a monthly, market-value weighted, trader-priced, total return index of domestic convertible bonds with a minimum principal outstanding of $50 million, domestic convertible preferred stocks with a minimum of 500,00 shares outstanding, and Eurodollar convertible bonds with a minimum principal outstanding of $100 million issued by U.S. corporations. All securities rated by Standard and Poor's Corporation must have a B-minimum rating. The index contains nearly 300 issues. Securities which fall below the selection criteria of the index are held in the index until the end of the year, after which they are deleted. Issues called for redemption are deleted at month's end unless the call date falls in the first ten days of the month. New issues are added to the index at the beginning of the month following issuance.

The Goldman Sachs Convertible 100 is a monthly, equal-weighted, trader-priced, total return index of convertible bonds with

Exhibit 2-7. Selection Criteria and Characteristics of High Yield Indexes

(as of 12/31/89)

	First Boston High Yield	*Salomon Composite High Yield*	*Merrill Lynch High Yield Master*	*DLJ High Yield Active Issue Index*	*Lehman Brothers High Yield Index*
Minimum Size at Issue (million)	$100 - 1 mo. seasoning $250 - immediately	50	25	None 225 is smallest	None
Minimum Rating	None	Caa/CCC for entry D for exit	C3/C-	B-	None D for exit
Maximum Rating	Ba1/BB+	BB+	Ba1/BB+	BB+	Ba1
Minimum Maturity	1 year	7 yrs.	1 year	None	None
Subjective Criteria	Exclude if never trades or <5 institutions hold	Liquidity	None	Trader opinion of liquidity	Liquidity
Market Value (billion)	73.8	54.8	97.7	8.9	50.4
Number of Issues	342	318	803	20	297
Weighting of Issues	Market value	Market value	Market value	Duration	Market Value
Pricing (i.e., Trader, Matrix)	Trader/monthly	Trader/monthly	Matrix/daily	Trader/weekly	Trader/monthly

a minimum principal amounting outstanding of $100 million and convertible preferred issues with a minimum market value outstanding of $100 million. With 100 issues in the index, it represents about 33 percent of the market value of all convertible securities outstanding. Securities are substituted following mergers, redemptions, and new issuance; no rating restrictions are used to select the issues. It should be noted that in selecting the securities for this index, an attempt is made to maintain industry sector diversification and some industry symmetry with the Standard & Poor's 500 Equity Index.

The Merrill Lynch Convertible Master Index is a daily, market-value weighted, trader- and matrix-priced, total return index of some 600 convertible bonds with a minimum principal amount outstanding of $25 million each. The index includes U.S. domestic convertible bonds, Eurodollar convertible bonds issued by U.S. corporations and U.S. domestic convertible preferred stocks. Bankrupt issues and issues convertible into cash, bonds, or preferred stocks as a result of mergers are excluded from the index.

The Froley Revy Convertible Bond Index consists of a smaller universe of 30 convertible bonds; the specific issues, which are equal-weighted in the index, are selected by Froley, Revy Investment Company, Inc. on the basis of liquidity, size, and representation of the diversity of the convertible bond market. Issues are replaced either as their premium increases beyond 66.67 percent or their price increases to $130 or above. Issues also are replaced as a result of bankruptcies, redemptions or mergers.

To date, most index funds have been designed to track indexes that comprise traditional sectors of the market such as Treasury, agency, corporate and mortgage-backed securities. This focus has been driven by the larger size of those market sectors and by their widespread acceptance as viable and prudent investment alternatives to active investment advisors. In specialized market sectors, particularly in the high yield and convertible bond sectors, investors expect investment advisors to add value through security selection and fundamental research. It is unlikely, therefore, that indexing will be considered a viable alternative to active investment advisors.

Customized Indexes

A customized index is designed to meet the specific requirements and objectives of an investor with a given risk tolerance and investment horizon. Customized indexes also can be designed to conform with any regulations that constrain an investor.

Interest in customized indexes has grown significantly since 1986. Several large public funds have selected customized indexes with durations that are longer than the durations of the broad market indexes and with greater weighting of corporate and mortgage-backed securities. Many large corporate pension plan sponsors have selected customized long-duration indexes that match the duration of their pension liability schedules. The growing interest in customized indexes can be attributed to at least six developments:

- Increasingly, the investment community recognizes that funds have different long-term objectives and risk preferences, and that all funds need not have the same total return performance and volatility of returns as those of a broad market index. The requirements and objectives of an endowment fund, for example, are not the same as those of an overfunded large pension plan. Consequently, the performance of the two funds should not be evaluated using a single broad market index.
- Financial Accounting Standards Board Statements 87 and 88 (FASB 87) have introduced new pension accounting requirements, some of which became mandatory in as early as 1987. FASB 87 imposes new standards for calculating and reporting both pension expenses on income statements and also pension liabilities in excess of the market value of pension plan assets on balance sheets. The new standards require the use of market interest rates, thereby introducing market-related volatility to the income statement and to the balance sheet as interest rates fluctuate from one reporting period to another. The interest in controlling market-related volatility of the pension expenses and in maintaining stable and favorable asset-liability ratios has prompted many corporate pension

plan sponsors to index pension assets against a customized index that fluctuates with their liabilities.

- The ban on incentive fees (which tie the compensation of investment advisors to their performance relative to an index) was removed by the SEC in November 1985 and by the Department of Labor (which regulates the employee pension industry through the Employee Retirement Security Act of 1974, or ERISA) in August 1986. The successful implementation of incentive fees, however, depends on the selection of an appropriate index that suits the needs of the client paying the incentive fees and adequately compensates the investment advisor. Often, a customized index is designed to incorporate accurately all of the constraints imposed on the investment advisor and to satisfy both the client and the investment advisor. A normal portfolio which reflects the investment style of an investment advisor is, in fact, a type of customized index.
- Investment advisors offering index fund management have sought to establish market niches by promoting their specific services and capabilities in the design and use of customized indexes. The efforts of investment advisors have prompted many investors to specify in great detail, and therefore increasingly to control, the level of interest rate risk, sector risk, and credit risk assumed by their portfolios.
- Investment advisors sometimes can command higher fees for managing index funds based on customized indexes than for funds based on generic broad market indexes or sub-indexes.
- Members of the broker/dealer community design and promote customized indexes in an effort to increase market share and the concomitant trading activity in the index and index-related products. Salomon Brothers Inc. introduced its Large Pension Fund Baseline Bond Index in December 1986 as a standardized, customized index designed specifically for large, long-term-oriented pension funds. This index was adopted by the California State Teachers Retirement System in August 1987 as the benchmark for indexing some $13.0

billion. In August 1987, Salomon Brothers Inc. introduced a matrix of indexes designed to allow customization of indexes by providing a means of selecting among different duration levels and market sector weightings.

Designing and Monitoring A Customized Index

The first step in designing a customized index is to specify the fund's objectives. Maximizing long-term expected return, producing a minimum annual real rate of return, matching liabilities, maximizing liquidity, preserving capital, and maintaining favorable asset-liability ratios are popular objectives among investors. Some of these objectives are short-term, while others are long-term. In addition, investors also may specify different levels of risk tolerance.

The most important and certainly the most difficult task in designing a customized index is translating these broad and sweeping objectives into concrete goals and risk parameters. Often, non-financial considerations have to be incorporated into the design as well. Some public pension funds, for example, have required indexes that excluded securities of corporations involved in business in South Africa.

The second step in the design process is to determine a duration (and maturity distribution) and a sector distribution for the index that can best meet the fund's objectives. The duration of the customized index can be tied either to that of a broad market index or to that of a particular liability schedule. Alternatively, the duration can be set at an absolute level. For example, some plan sponsors specify long-duration indexes as a deflationary hedge.

A critical decision is whether to design a fixed- (or constant-) duration index or a floating- (or interest-rate-sensitive-) duration index in which duration changes in response to changes in interest rates. In traditional indexes such as the Salomon BIG Index and its components, the Lehman Aggregate Index and its components, and the Merrill Domestic Master and its components, duration increases as interest rates fall and decreases as interest rates rise. More recently, however, there has been some interest in designing customized indexes with a duration that is maintained at a fixed level regardless of the change in interest rates. Maintaining a fixed duration requires rebalancing the index by adding or deleting securities to bring the index duration in line with the original target duration. The frequency of rebalancing can vary from as often as daily changes to monthly or quarterly changes. The frequency of rebalancing also can be a function of the magnitude of deviation of the index duration from its target duration. For example, if interest rates fall significantly in a short period thereby increasing the duration of the index above the target duration by a certain magnitude, some long-term Treasury securities in the index can be deleted to reduce the index duration to its initial target.

Once the duration has been selected, investors have to decide on a sector distribution. The sector distribution determines the weightings assigned to government securities, corporate securities and mortgage-backed securities. Plan sponsors seeking the higher yields from corporate bonds and mortgage-backed securities (Exhibits 2-8 and 2-9) may choose to overweight these two sectors relative to their actual distribution in the market. Other sponsors may be averse to the risk of exposure to adverse spread movements between corporate and mortgage-backed securities on the one hand, and government securities on the other. The significant deterioration in credit quality (Exhibit 2-10) over the last few years may also discourage some investors from seeking the higher yields of corporate bonds. Finally, sponsors with large liquidity requirements may choose to overweight Treasuries.

Once the key parameters of a customized index are set, the next step is to advise the investor of the expected performance of the index under alternative market scenarios. If a short-duration index is selected, the plan sponsor should be informed of the expected underperformance of this index relative to the broad market indexes in a period of falling interest rates. Similarly, if corporate bonds are overweighted, the index will underperform as spreads between corporate and government securities widen. Such a risk may be acceptable to some investors and consistent with their funds' long-term objectives; nonetheless, these types of risks must be spelled out clearly.

Exhibit 2-8. 30-Year A-Rated Industrials vs. 30-Year Treasury (12/31/78 to 12/31/89)

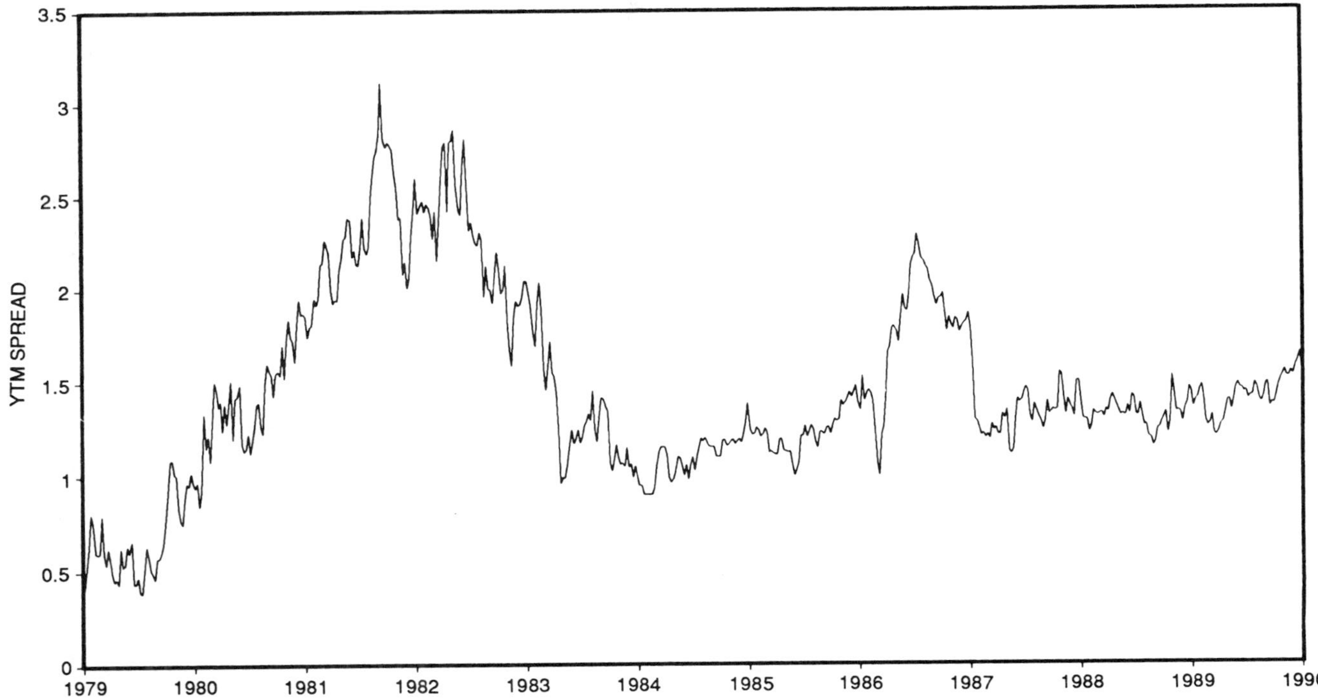

Source: The First Boston Corporation.

Exhibit 2-9. Current Coupon GNMA's vs. 10-Year Treasury (12/31/78 to 12/31/89) (Yield Spread in Basis Points)

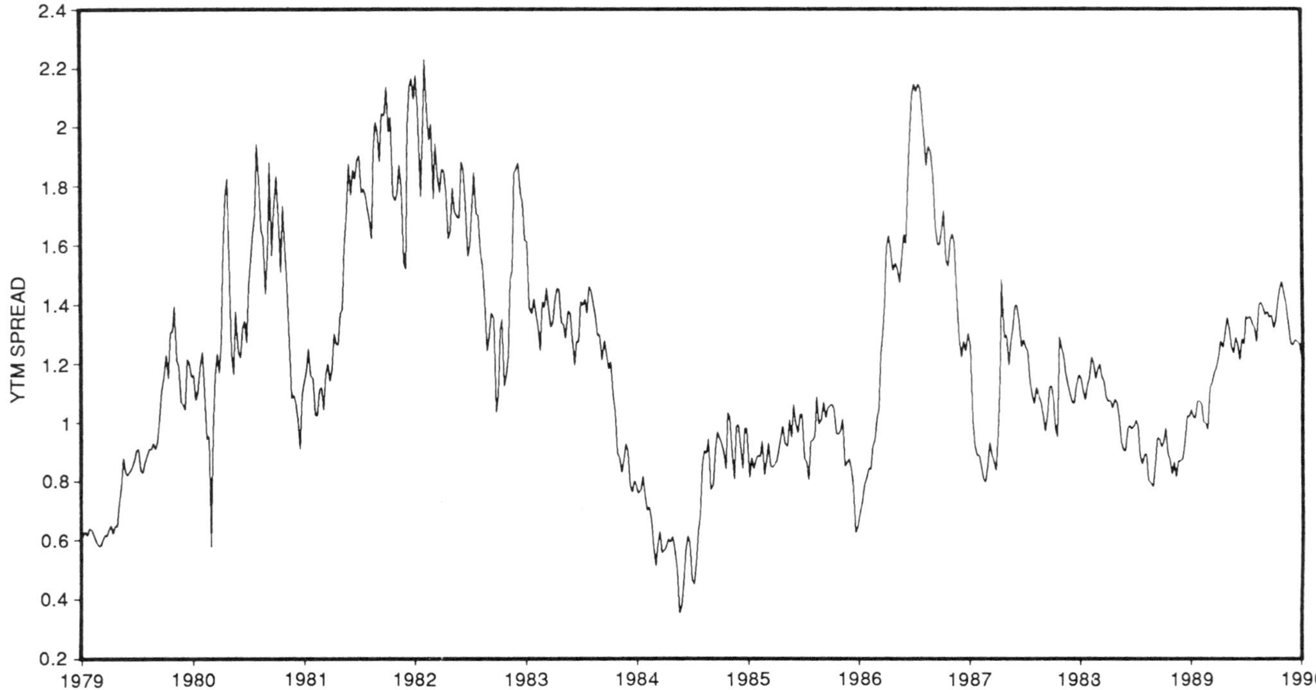

Source: The First Boston Corporation.

Exhibit 2-10. Changes in Credit Quality: Upgrades vs. Downgrades*

	1982	*1983*	*1984*	*1985*	*1986*	*1987*	*1988*	*1989*
No. of Upgrades	49	91	161	124	143	100	142	138
No. of Downgrades	169	149	148	153	246	176	237	339
Downgrades as Percent of Total	77.5%	62.1%	47.9%	55.2%	63.2%	63.8%	62.5%	71.1%

*Investment-grade and high yield fixed income issuers.

Source: Moody's Investor Services.

This type of scenario analysis can be complemented by a review of the historical return and risk levels of the customized index. An historical review advances the plan sponsor's understanding of the index and provides useful insights into the impact of various duration and sector biases.

The last step in the design of a customized index is to set up an information system for monitoring the index. The performance and characteristics of customized indexes can be measured in several ways. The most simple and direct approach is to use various sub-indexes of publicly-available indexes and to weight each sub-index in order to obtain the desired duration and sector distribution. The sub-indexes should be monitored regularly to ensure that the characteristics of the customized index are consistent with the initial objectives of the investor, and that the customized index remains a practical and replicable benchmark. There are two disadvantages to this approach. First, the investors and the index fund advisors are dependent on the producers of the sub-indexes for their design and maintenance. And second, the type of customized index that can be designed is limited by the sub-indexes that are publicly available.

An alternative and more precise approach is to use a database of fixed-income securities to select a universe of securities which, when aggregated, provide the duration and sector distribution required for the customized index. The securities can be selected based on various criteria such as minimum or maximum maturity, minimum quality, or minimum size outstanding. The selected universe of securities then can be used to generate the necessary information on the performance and characteristics of a customized index. One of the problems with this approach is the amount of resources required to maintain such a database; the answer is to work with one of the major broker/dealers or research boutiques which already have such databases and to use their resources to maintain customized indexes.

Three common pitfalls should be avoided when designing a customized index. A customized index must not be unduly complex in terms of types of securities included in the index or the index structure. A complex index may lead to unreliable pricing, unrealistic constraints, and impractical assumptions. An index must also avoid high turnover of securities in its universe since high turnover will result in high turnover in the index itself and consequently in higher transaction costs for the fund. For example, a barbelled index with one-to-two-year maturity range at the short end of the barbell will lead to a 100 percent turnover of assets for that portion of the index every year. Finally, the criteria for selecting securities for a customized index must be objective to prevent any misunderstanding of why particular securities or sectors were included in or excluded from the index.

SELECTING THE INDEX PRODUCER

Once the type of index—broad market, sub-index, specialized market sector, or customized—has been selected, the next step is to choose a producer for that index. Currently, indexes are produced by the research departments of large broker/dealers, by small research boutiques or investment advisory firms, and by purveyors of financial information services. Exhibit 2-11 lists the key producers of fixed income indexes.

There are several considerations in selecting an index producer that impact the effectiveness of the investment advisor in managing an index fund. The form in which data on the index is made available is one such consideration. Data is available in three forms. The most useful form—and the most expensive to generate—is an on-line information system through which users of the index have complete flexibility in accessing the data at any level of detail, manipulating the data, interacting with the software to produce customized indexes and comparing portfolios to appropriate indexes. Currently, Lehman Brothers Inc. is the only producer of indexes providing such access and flexibility.

A second form is on-line access, but with limited ability to manipulate the data and compare portfolios to indexes. Merrill Lynch Capital Markets provides data on its indexes in this form through "The Bloomberg."

The third form in which data is made available is printed material, including periodic—usually monthly—reports on the indexes

Exhibit 2-11. Producers of Indexes

Type of Index / *Producers*	*Broad Market*	*Sub-index*	*Specialized Market Sector*	*Customized*
Salomon Brothers Inc.	BIG	Gov't., Corp., MBS, et. al.	High Yields, STRIPS	(available)
Lehman Brothers Inc.	Aggregate	Gov't., Corp., MBS, et. al.	—	(available)
Merrill Lynch Capital Markets	Domestic Master	Gov't., Corp., MBS, et. al.	High Yield, Convert-ibles, TIGR, STRIPS	(available)
Morgan Stanley & Co. Inc.	—	Mortgage-Backed Securities	—	—
Goldman Sachs & Co.	—	—	Convertible	—
Froley, Revy Investment Company Inc.	—	—	Convertible	—
First Boston Corporation	—	—	High Yield, Convertible	—
Payden and Rygel	—	—	Money Market and Short Maturity	—
Ryan Labs	—	On-the-Run Treasuries	GIC	(available)
Donaldson Lufkin & Jenrette	—	—	Zero Coupon, High Yield	—

and their characteristics. This form is the least useful to the index fund advisor due to only limited access to the data. It is, however, most beneficial to the producer of the index since, in effect, it renders the index fund advisor completely dependent on the producer of the index for any data manipulation, portfolio comparison, and selection of securities for purchase or sale. Such increased dependence typically results in greater trading activity between the index fund advisor and the index producer.

Another consideration in selecting an index producer is the level and timeliness of support provided to the index fund advisor by the producer. At least in principle, the frequency of data, the speed with which information is updated, and the quality and timeliness of responses to questions and project requests all affect the performance or effectiveness of an index fund advisor.

Chapter 3

Setting Up and Managing Index Funds

Index funds are designed to match the total return of a particular basket of securities, e.g., the index. Clearly, the most direct and fail-safe approach to setting up an index fund would be to purchase all securities contained in the selected index in the same proportion as they are held in that index. But this approach is not a feasible one in the case of fixed income funds.

First, most fixed income indexes contain thousands of securities; investing in all those securities in the appropriate proportion would result in an index fund whose holdings of each security are too small for portfolio rebalancing and future trading. Portfolio rebalancing is necessary as income generated by the index fund is reinvested and as securities with less than one year remaining to maturity drop out of the index. Additional trading is necessary as well because new Treasury, agency, corporate, and mortgage-backed securities are continuously issued and added to the index and other securities are removed from the index.

Second, a significant portion of all securities contained in bond indexes are illiquid, i.e., they cannot be purchased readily in the secondary market. In some cases, the illiquidity is attributed to defeasance programs in which bonds are permanently placed in a trust for the purpose of satisfying or "defeasing" a given cash flow schedule. Such bonds are, in effect, taken out of the market. In other instances, illiquidity is attributed to the placement of securities in portfolios with limited trading activity, such as dedicated (or immunized) portfolios, large index funds, and large insurance company portfolios. Since trading in the fixed income market occurs on an "over-the-counter" basis rather than in a centralized exchange with specialists, identifying the owners of such securities and purchasing the securities at a reasonable market price is very difficult, if not impossible.

The more practical approach to setting up an index fund is to select a basket of securities whose aggregated profile characteristics (such as portfolio yield, effective duration, and convexity) and expected total return match those of the index. Three methodologies are available for selecting and maintaining the appropriate basket: the stratified sampling approach; the optimization approach using linear programming; and the optimization approach using quadratic programming. All three methodologies are used widely.

This chapter examines these methodologies and evaluates their advantages and disadvantages. The chapter also reviews the suitability of each approach depending on type of benchmark, size of index fund, level of experience of the index fund manager and extent of resources available to the index fund manager. Finally, the chapter discusses the rebalancing requirements for managing an index fund.

Stratified Sampling

The stratified sampling method, also known as the "cellular" approach, is the most simple and flexible of the three approaches. In stratified sampling, an index is divided into subsectors, i.e., the index is stratified into cells. The division into subsectors is made on the basis of such parameters as sector, coupon, term-to-maturity, duration, and quality. Additionally, the index can be divided into either broad or detailed subsectors.

Exhibit 3-1 illustrates the division of a market index into broad subsectors or cells. Two parameters are used to divided the index, namely sector and term-to-maturity (or weighted average life for mortgage-backed securities). The division by sector stratifies the market index into government, mortgage-backed, corporate, and Yankee securities; the division by term-to-maturity stratifies the market index into securities with terms-to-maturity of between one and five years, between five and ten years, and greater than ten years. Under this stratification, the market index is divided into 12 cells and all securities in the index fall into one of those cells. For example, all government securities with terms-to-maturity greater than or equal to five years and less than ten years fall into the fifth cell. It should be noted that the number of cells—12 in this example—is the product of the number of sectors and the number of term-to-maturity ranges (i. e., 4 × 3 = 12).

Typically, however, a market index is divided into detailed subsectors. Using sector and term-to-maturity parameters again, the division by sector could stratify the market index into Treasuries and agencies instead of government securities; into Ginnie Maes, Fannie Maes, Freddie Macs, and their 15-year original issue counter-

Exhibit 3-1. Stratification into Broad Cells: Sector and Term-to-Maturity*

Sectors / Term-to-Maturity	*Governments*	*Mortgage-Backed Securities*	*Corporates*	*Yankees*
1–5	Cell 1	Cell 2	Cell 3	Cell 4
5–10	Cell 5	Cell 6	Cell 7	Cell 8
10+	Cell 9	Cell 10	Cell 11	Cell 12

*Weighted Average Life For Mortgage-Backed Securities

parts (Midgets, Dwarfs, Gnomes, and non-Gnome 15-year FHLMCs) and project loans instead of mortgage-backed securities; into industrial, utility, telephone, finance, and transportation securities instead of corporate securities; and into Canadian, World Bank, sovereign, and supra-national securities instead of Yankee securities. The division by term-to-maturity could stratify the market index into, say, two-year intervals where the first interval includes all securities with terms-to-maturity between one and three years. A commonly used division by term-to-maturity stratifies the market index into two- or three-year intervals for the first ten years (one to three years, three to five years, five to seven years and seven to ten years), and five-year intervals thereafter (ten to 15 years, 15 to 20 years, 20 to 25 years and greater than 25 years).

Divisions are made also on the basis of coupon. Exhibit 3-2 is an example of a detailed division by sector and coupon; the division by coupon has stratified the market index into two-percent intervals. In this exhibit, the index is divided into 66 cells, where the first cell contains all Treasury securities that have coupon levels below six percent. The last cell contains all Yankee securities that have coupon levels equal to or greater than 14 percent. It should be noted that, ultimately, an index can be divided into as many cells as there are issues in the index so that each cell contains only one issue.

The stratification of the index is followed by the selection of securities to represent each cell. Securities are chosen so that the profile characteristics and the expected total return of each "sample" of securities representing a particular cell match the average characteristics and expected total return of all securities in that cell. Each cell may be treated differently. In some cases, the average characteristics of the cell are matched; in other cases, cells which account for a large percentage of the index may be stratified further into "sub-cells." And still in other cases, cells that represent a nominal percentage of the index may be omitted from the index fund altogether. Of the factors that determine the number of cells and sub-categories in an index fund, the size of the fund is the most critical. A large asset size enables the index fund manager to divide the benchmark into greater number of cells and to select samples of securities that represent most of the cells in the index.

Exhibit 3-2. Stratification into Detailed Cells: Sector and Coupon

Coupon \ Sector	*Treasury*	*Agency*	*GNMA*	*FNMA*	*FHLMC*	*15-Year MBS*	*Project Loan*	*Indus-trial*	*Finance*	*Utility*	*Yankee*	*Total*
Less than 6	Cell 1											
6–7.99												
8–9.99												
10–11.99												
12–13.99												
14+											Cell 66	
Total												

Exhibit 3-3. Stratification into Detailed Cells: Sector and Term-to-Maturity*

Sector / Term-to-Maturity	*Treasury*	*Agency*	*GNMA*	*FNMA*	*FHLMC*	*15-Year MBS*	*Project*	*Indus-trial*	*Finance*	*Utility*	*Yankee*	*Total*
Less than 3	17.14% 7.76% 1.67 yrs.		0.02% 9.45% 0.80 yrs.									
3 – 5												
5 – 7				1.39% 10.13% 4.25 yrs.								
7 – 10												
10 – 15		0.05% 9.64% 5.88 yrs.										
15 – 30										3.32% 10.47% 5.98 yrs.		
30+												
Total												

*Weighted Average Life for Mortgage-Backed Securities

Key:

Percent of index Average yield Avg. effective duration

Source: Salomon Brothers Inc.

Exhibit 3-3 represents a detailed stratification by sector and term-to-maturity of a broad market index. Five cells have been highlighted: Cells 1, 3, 26, 46, and 65. Each cell's share of the market value of the index, and each cell's average yield and average effective duration is shown. The first cell accounts for the largest share of the market value of the index, or 17.14 percent. This cell includes all Treasury securities with term-to-maturity greater than or equal to one and less than three years, and has an average yield of 7.76 percent and effective duration of 1.67 years. Because the cell represents the largest component of the index relative to other cells (and also the largest component of the index fund), it is stratified further.

Exhibit 3-4 represents the further stratification of the first cell by coupon. This type of secondary stratification is important in determining the distribution of securities across coupon levels. For example, Treasury securities with coupon levels greater than or equal to six percent and less than eight percent account for the largest share of Cell 1, namely 51.87 percent; this level compares to a 3.34 percent share for Treasury securities with coupon levels greater than or equal to 14 percent. A 3.34 percent allocation accounts for the smallest share of Cell 1. In the index fund, therefore, Treasury securities with coupon levels between six and eight percent will represent a proportionally greater share than Treasury securities with coupon levels greater than or equal to 14 percent. Furthermore, of the Treasury securities with coupon levels between six and eight percent contained in Cell 1 of the index fund, nearly two-thirds will have maturities between one and 1.99 years (Sub-cell 1 in Exhibit 3-4 representing a percentage share of 35.39), and one-third will have maturities between two and 2.99 years (Sub-cell 6 in Exhibit 3-4 representing a percentage share of 16.48)

After further stratification, the next step is to choose the appropriate securities for the selected sub-cells in Exhibit 3-4. For example, the first sub-cell can be represented in an index fund with the following securities at an average yield and effective duration that closely match those of the sub-cell and are "fairly" valued in the market relative to alternative securities:

Exhibit 3-4. Secondary Stratification of Cell 1: Treasury Securities with term-to-maturity between 1 and 3 years

Term-to-Maturity \ Coupon	*6 – 7.99*	*8 – 9.99*	*10 – 11.99*	*12 – 13.99*	*14+*	*Total*
1 – 1.99	35.39% 7.66% 1.41 yrs.	14.25% 7.66% 1.41 yrs.	7.52% 7.61% 1.27 yrs.	3.63% 7.73% 1.52 yrs.	3.34% 7.42% 1.14 yrs.	64.13% 7.64% 1.39 yrs.
2 – 2.99	16.48% 7.94% 2.21 yrs.	7.25% 8.04% 2.38 yrs.	10.61% 7.93% 2.00 yrs.	1.53% 8.06% 2.38 yrs.	0% — —	35.87% 7.96% 2.19 yrs.
Total	51.87% 7.74% 1.66 yrs.	21.50% 7.78% 1.74 yrs.	18.13% 7.80% 1.70 yrs.	5.16% 7.83% 1.77 yrs.	3.34% 7.42% 1.14 yrs.	100.00% 7.76% 1.67 yrs.

Key:

Percent of cell 1 Average yield Avg. effective duration

Source: Salomon Brothers Inc.

	Effective Yield	Market Duration	Value Weight
1. U.S. Treasury 6.250 2/28/89	7.48%	1.09 Yrs.	20%
2. U.S. Treasury 7.625 7/31/89	7.64%	1.46 Yrs.	60%
3. U.S. Treasury 7.875 10/31/89	7.74%	1.67 Yrs.	20%
Average	7.63%	1.43 Yrs.	100%

The securities are weighted such that the average yield and effective duration of the three securities together approximate the 7.66 percent yield and 1.41-year effective duration of the sub-cell.

Cell 65 of the index representing utility securities with terms-to-maturity of between 15 and 30 years, also requires similar secondary stratification because it accounts for the single largest cell among corporate securities. The cell is further stratified by coupon and credit quality, as shown in Exhibit 3-5. Selecting securities to represent the sub-cells in Exhibit 3-5 is primarily a function of the availability in the over-the-counter market of securities that meet both the required characteristics such as term-to-maturity, coupon and quality, and the particular credit quality criteria of the index fund manager. There are about 870 utility securities with term-to-maturity of between 15 and 30 years. Some of the securities might not be selected due to their lack of marketability; for example, Canal Electric 8.85s of 9/01/06 with an amount outstanding of $34.65 million and Iowa Power and Light 8.25s of 9/15/07 with an amount outstanding of $29.70 million represent small issues and probably are unavailable in the secondary market.

Other securities like those issued by Philadelphia Electric Company might not be selected because of perceived deteriorating credit standing. On the other hand, securities issued by Duke Power Company might be selected because of both stable credit conditions as well as Duke Power Company's AA credit rating; securities with AA credit ratings account for 34.29 percent of Cell 65 as shown in Exhibit 3-5. Of the 12 Duke Power Company issues in Cell 65, the 9.00s of 5/1/16 is an appropriate selection. First, in the AA category, the sub-cell with coupons of between eight and 9.99 percent accounts for the largest share of Cell 65 and this issue falls in that

Exhibit 3-5. Secondary Stratification of Cell 65: Utility Securities with terms-to-maturity between 15 and 30 years

Credit Quality \ Coupon	*Less than 6*	*6 – 7.99*	*8 – 9.99*	*10 – 11.99*	*12 – 13.99*	*14+*	*Total*
AAA	0.24% 9.61% 9.02 yrs.	1.10% 9.71% 7.36 yrs.	2.97% 9.80% 6.65 yrs.	0.04% 10.05% 4.59 yrs.	0% — —	0% — —	4.34% 9.77% 6.94 yrs.
AA	0.96% 9.74% 8.85 yrs.	7.14% 9.78% 7.48 yrs.	21.46% 9.96% 6.24 yrs.	2.83% 10.48% 4.44 yrs.	1.69% 11.29% 2.51 yrs.	0.20% 14.16% 1.29 yrs.	34.29% 10.05% 6.21 yrs.
A		1.84% 9.87% 7.12 yrs.	17.97% 10.18% 6.30 yrs.	3.94% 10.48% 5.17 yrs.	2.66% 11.52% 3.12 yrs.	0.12% 12.79% 1.89 yrs.	26.54% 10.35% 5.85 yrs.
BBB		0.81% 10.33% 7.03 yrs.	16.74% 10.64% 6.44 yrs.	10.76% 11.18% 5.64 yrs.	5.89% 11.90% 3.97 yrs.	0.62% 13.81% 3.37 yrs.	34.83% 11.07% 5.74 yrs.
Total	1.20% 9.71% 8.88 yrs.	10.89% 9.83% 7.37 yrs.	59.15% 10.21% 6.33 yrs.	17.58% 10.91% 5.34 yrs.	10.24% 11.70% 3.51 yrs.	0.94% 13.76% 2.74 yrs.	100.00% 10.47% 5.98 yrs.

Key:

Percent of cell 65
Average yield
Avg. effective duration

Source: Salomon Brothers Inc.

sub-cell. Second, in Cell 56, Duke Power is the fourteenth largest issuer of utility securities.

It should be noted that all cells in this index are not stratified further into sub-cells. Where cells are too small for secondary stratification (such as Cell 26 in Exhibit 3-3 which contains Fannie Maes with weighted average lives of between five and seven years), the average yield and average effective duration of that cell are replicated by selecting a sample of securities whose average characteristics match those of the cell. In the case of those cells which represent a small fraction of the index, such as Cell 3 (which contains Ginnie Maes and Graduated Payment Mortgage-Backed Securities with weighted average lives less than three years and which accounts for 0.02 percent of the index) and Cell 46 (which contains agency securities with terms-to-maturity of between ten and 15 years and which accounts for 0.05 percent of the index), the cells are eliminated from the index fund. Selecting securities to represent these cells in a typical index fund, say with assets under $500 million, will result in portfolio holdings that are too small to be readily marketable.

The process of setting up an index fund is complete when all cells in the index have been either replicated (directly through matching average characteristics or indirectly after further stratification) or eliminated from the index fund. The process can take several hours, several weeks or even several months depending on the size of the fund and the type of index fund. For example, the $13 billion California State Teachers' Retirement System Index Fund designed to track the Salomon Brothers Large Pension Fund Baseline Bond Index would benefit from a selective purchase of corporate and seasoned mortgage-backed securities; typically, such selective purchases cannot be made in a short period. In such instances, index fund managers often purchase Treasury securities to match the duration and the maturity distribution of the index, and then phase in the purchase of corporate and seasoned mortgage-backed securities based on availability and relative value.

On the other hand, a large index fund designed to match a Treasury index requires less time to construct due to a greater liquidity in the secondary market for Treasury securities. For example, a $500 million Treasury index fund could be set up in a matter of hours, although many investment managers prefer to phase in the purchase of securities for any type of portfolio, expecting to obtain a lower average price for setting up the portfolio.

As noted earlier, one of the key advantages of the stratified sampling approach is its simplicity. Stratifying an index into cells and selecting securities to represent each cell does not require sophisticated index-related analytical systems, extensive databases on security prices and dealer inventory, or even strong quantitative expertise. In fact, a thorough understanding of the cellular structure of an index, a working knowledge of spread sheet software, and a security and portfolio review system to evaluate security and portfolio characteristics are sufficient. Unlike the linear programming and quadratic programming approaches, stratified sampling relies on portfolio management expertise to stratify the index appropriately, to eliminate unnecessary cells, to substitute one cell for another and to select a basket of securities that will closely track the index.

Another important advantage of stratified sampling is flexibility. This methodology is effective with all types of indexes. For example, stratified sampling is as effective with a mortgage-backed securities index fund as it is with a Treasury securities index fund. Specific mortgage-backed pools can be selected to represent the cells containing seasoned Freddie Mac and Fannie Mae securities. In both the linear programming and the quadratic programming approaches, mortgage-backed securities are selected based on the aggregate or generic characteristics of a large number of mortgage-backed pools with similar coupons and original terms-to-maturity.

Similarly, stratified sampling is equally useful for managing a passive "vanilla" index fund and an actively managed enhanced index fund. For example, securities in an actively managed enhanced index fund are often traded on a continuous basis. In stratified sampling, securities in a cell can be easily swapped without impacting the structure of the index fund; in a true optimization using linear or quadratic programming, the impact of every swap has to be evaluated and the portfolio re-optimized. Furthermore, investment strategies designed to enhance portfolio returns (Chapter 5) can be implemented more easily in stratified sampling, i.e., yield and convexity tilts can be targeted to particular sectors. Convexity can be maximized in some of the Treasury cells, while yield can be maximized in some of the corporate cells. In the optimization approach using linear programming, on the other hand, yield and convexity tilts are imposed at the aggregate level on the entire portfolio rather than on specific cells.

Finally, stratified sampling lends itself to the use of securities that are not included in the index. Securities with complex structures such as derivative mortgage-backed securities can be substituted for generic mortgage-backed securities in an index fund. However, evaluating both derivative securities and the appropriateness of specific substitutions requires proper judgment and a range of assumptions. Such trade-specific judgments and assumptions cannot be incorporated practically in the two optimization approaches.

Its simplicity and flexibility notwithstanding, stratified sampling does have certain shortcomings. Stratified sampling is labor-intensive. A portfolio manager must determine the ideal cellular structure for an index based on size of portfolio and type of benchmark. The manager then must evaluate the trade-offs between eliminating some cells and including others. Finally, the manager must select securities for each cell while controlling the overall characteristics of the index fund. Such investment decisions require both time and experience in managing index funds.

Another problem associated with stratified sampling is the risk of introducing unintended biases to the index fund. For example, while focusing on market sector weights, a portfolio manager may deviate inadvertently from the maturity distribution of the index; intermediate maturity securities may be overweighted, and short- and long-term maturity securities may be underweighted relative to the index. Such a deviation can evade notice if the average maturity and effective duration of the portfolio remain unchanged. Undoubtedly, the likelihood of this type of error is greater with stratified sampling than with optimization approaches. However, it should be noted that an experienced index fund manager would minimize the risk of such errors by monitoring the maturity distribution of the index and the index fund as well as by tracking the index fund's structure through a number of reports that highlight the difference between an index and its corresponding fund.

Exhibit 3-6 is an example of such a report. This report measures the difference in market value share, yield and effective duration of each cell between the index and the index fund. A value of zero for the first item in each cell signifies a match in market value share between the index and the index fund, a negative number means the index fund is underweighted in that cell and a positive number signifies an overweighting. Therefore, the first zeros in each cell of the last row indicate that the market value share of each sector in the index fund matches the index, i.e., no particular sector has been overweighted or underweighted.

Similarly, a value of zero for the second and third item in each cell signifies a match between the index and the index fund of the yield and effective duration of each cell, respectively; negative numbers mean lower yields and effective durations in the index fund, and positive numbers mean higher yields and effective durations. For example, in the last row of Exhibit 3-6, a positive 0.22 percent in the corporate and Yankees sector indicates that the corporates and Yankees contained in the index fund together have higher average yield than the average of those in the index. This yield tilt is occurring in the corporates and Yankees with maturities greater than or equal to five years. Such a yield bias may be a result of specific undervalued issues selected by the portfolio manager or of a slight overweighting of lower credit quality securities.

The last row in this report also indicates a difference in the effective duration of the government and mortgage-backed sectors of the index fund relative to the index. The effective duration of the government sector in the index fund is longer than the duration index by 0.19 years. Because the government sector accounts for 55.33 percent of the index fund, the 0.19-year difference in duration translates into a 0.10-year increase in the duration of the entire index fund. This increase in duration is offset by a shorter effective duration in the mortgage-backed securities sector of 0.41 years. Because the mortgage-backed securities sector accounts for 25.48 percent of the index fund, the 0.41-year difference in duration translates into a 0.10-year decrease in the duration of the index fund. These

Exhibit 3-6. Structural Difference Between Index Fund and Index: Sector and Term-to-Maturity

Term-to-Maturity* / Sector	Governments	Mortgage-Backed Securities	Corporates and Yankees	Total
1 – 5	30.58% 0.00 0.00 0.00	2.28% 0.00 0.00 0.00	4.32% 0.00 0.00 0.00	37.17% 0.00 0.00 0.00
5 – 10	12.60% 0.00 0.00 0.00	17.69% 0.00 0.00 -0.59 yrs.	5.09% 0.00 0.15% 0.00	35.38% 0.00 0.00 -0.29 yrs.
10+	12.16% 0.00 0.00 0.86 yrs.	5.52% 0.00 0.00 0.00	9.77% 0.00 0.35% 0.00	27.44% 0.00 0.12% 0.38 yrs.
Total	55.33% 0.00 0.00 0.19 yrs.	25.48% 0.00 0.00 -0.41 yrs.	19.19% 0.00 0.22% 0.00	100% 0.00 0.04% 0.00

*Weighted Average Life For Mortgage-Backed Securities

Key:

	Market value share
Difference in market value share (%) Difference in yield (%) Difference in effective duration (yrs.)	

Source: Salomon Brothers Inc. for market value share of cells.

differences in duration can contribute to a measurable difference in returns between the index and the index fund. For example, if yield spreads between mortgage-backed securities and Treasury securities narrowed, the index fund will underperform the index in spite of identical market value shares in mortgage-backed securities. The underperformance is attributed to the lower duration of the index fund per dollar invested in the mortgage-backed securities sector.

In stratified sampling, such reports are critical to minimizing the risk of introducing inadvertent tilts and biases in the index fund. The reports can be designed to monitor sector and term-to-maturity biases (shown in Exhibit 3-6), as well as credit quality, coupon, and effective duration biases. Moreover, each cell in the reports can measure differences not only in market value share, average yield and effective duration between the index and index fund (shown in Exhibit 3-6), but also differences in other characteristics such as par value share, average effective yield, average nominal duration, contribution to aggregate portfolio duration, average coupon, average maturity, and average quality.

Finally, stratified sampling may not result in an optimal portfolio. A portfolio is optimal when it achieves the highest yield and greatest convexity for a given portfolio structure with respect to such parameters as maturity, coupon, quality, sector, and call exposure. Barring any issue-specific risks, an index fund that has a higher yield and equal convexity (or equal yield and greater convexity) will outperform its benchmark over time given the same portfolio structure. However, it is difficult, if not impossible, for an index fund manager using only stratified sampling to implement the optimal trade-offs between the yield and convexity of all securities held in the index fund—and of all those offered in the market—while maintaining the target portfolio structure.

Optimization Approach Using Linear Programming

The key shortcomings of stratified sampling—the extensive administrative demands on an index fund manager's time, the risk of inadvertent biases in the index fund, and the sub-optimal trade-offs between yield and convexity—can be overcome through a more systematic and mechanistic approach to dividing an index into cells, to selecting a basket of securities to represent those cells, and, importantly, to concurrently minimizing the differences in all cell characteristics between the index and the index fund. The optimization approach to indexing based on linear programming is one such comprehensive technique. This optimization is, in fact, a more disciplined and quantitative extension of stratified sampling. The purpose of any optimization using linear programming is to maximize the expected utility that is derived when allocating scarce resources among alternative and competing uses. Mathematically, the problem can be described as the selection of non-negative values for given variables, subject to a set of linear constraints on the values of those variables so as to maximize a given linear function. The given function is called the objective function.[1]

Applying this optimization approach to fixed income indexing, the goal can be restated as maximizing the likelihood that an index fund will track an index closely by allocating a finite number of dollars—the scarce resources—among the thousands of fixed income securities—the alternative and competing uses—available in the fixed income market. The linear programming problem is formulated by specifying three components: an objective function that, when maximized, increases the likelihood that an index fund will track its benchmark closely; a set of constraints that incorporate the target cellular structure of an index fund; and a universe of securities, also known as the opportunity set, from which a basket of securities can be selected.

The parameter represented by the objective function can vary among different optimization problems. Objective functions based on yield measures are the most widely used. In some problems, the par value-weighted yield-to-maturity of the portfolio is maximized; in others, the market value-weighted yield-to-maturity is maximized. Some optimizations may maximize the par-or market-value-

1. For a discussion on optimization and linear programming see Intriligator, Michael D., *Mathematical Optimization and Economic Theory* (New Jersey: Prentice-Hall, Inc., 1971), and Luenberger, David G., *Introduction to Linear and Nonlinear Programming* (Massachusetts: Addison-Wesley Publishing Company, 1973).

weighted effective yield to account for the call exposure of corporate securities and prepayment exposure of mortgage-backed securities. And still in other instances, a par or market value-weighted adjusted yield may be maximized; the yield adjustments are designed to account for the factors specific to each security including the amount outstanding of each security, sinking fund or special redemption features, coupon levels, and liquidity premiums. Objective functions also may be based on the expected return of the portfolio given a probability weighting of different interest rate scenarios, or on the par- or market-value-weighted convexity of the portfolio. These parameters typically are used when the index fund manager anticipates a particular change in interest rates or in the volatility of interest rates.

In all the optimizations, the objective function is of linear form, irrespective of the parameter that is maximized:

$$F(X) = c_1x_1 + c_2x_2 \ldots + c_nx_n$$

or

$$\sum_{i=1}^{n} c_ix_i$$

where

c_i is the parameter of each security i that is maximized, e.g., yield,

x_i determines the par amount selected of security i, and can be the par or market value, or the par or market value weighting of security i,

n represents the number of different securities in the universe from which the optimization will select securities.

The second component that must be specified is a set of constraints. The majority of constraints in the optimization problem define the cellular structure of the index fund. For example, in Exhibit 3-3, 17.14 percent of the index is represented by the first cell containing all Treasury securities with maturities of less than three years. This percentage share is matched in the index fund by using a constraint that specifies that the market value weighting in the index fund of all Treasury securities with maturities of less than three years must equal 17.14 percent.

It should be noted that because constraints with exact percentages are too restrictive, most optimization problems specify a range for the market value weight of each cell. In this example, two constraints can be used to specify an upper and lower bound for the range, say, 18.8 percent and 15.4 percent respectively, such that the market value of the cell is greater than or equal to 15.4 percent and less than or equal to 18.8 percent. Sometimes, two constraints may not be necessary because either the upper or the lower bound affect the solution of the optimization problem. If, for example, effective yield is maximized, a lower bound constraint on the market value of the corporate sector does not "bind" the solution and, therefore, becomes redundant. The constraints are expressed as linear inequalities:

$$
\begin{aligned}
a_{11}x_1 + a_{12}x_2 + \ldots + a_{1n}x_n &\geq b_1 \\
a_{21}x_1 + a_{22}x_2 + \ldots + a_{2n}x_n &\geq b_2 \\
\cdot \qquad\qquad &\quad \cdot \\
\cdot \qquad\qquad &\quad \cdot \\
\cdot \qquad\qquad &\quad \cdot \\
a_{m1}x_1 + a_{m2}x_2 + \ldots + a_{mn}x_n &\geq b_m
\end{aligned}
$$

or

$$\sum_{i=1}^{n} a_{ji}x_i \geq b_j \qquad \text{for } j = 1, 2, \ldots m$$

where a_{ji} is a constant with a value that depends on how x_i is defined in the objective function. For example, if x_i is defined as the par value of security i, then a_{ji} is the price of security i divided by the market value of cell j such that the sum of $a_{ji}x_i$ represents the market value weight of all securities in cell j. If, on the other hand, x_i is the market value weight of security i, then a_{ji} is zero when x_i is not contained in cell j and one when x_i is contained in cell j. B_j is an upper or lower bound for the market value weight of cell j. If the inequality represents an upper bound such that the sum of $a_{ji}x_i$ must be less than or equal to the upper bound, the inequality is multiplied by minus one.

A constraint is not specified for each cell. Cells that comprise a very small percentage of the index, such as Cell 3 (0.22 percent market value weighting) and Cell 46 (0.05 percent market value weighting) in Exhibit 3-3, are not included in the set of constraints. In fact, the cells that are eliminated from the index fund in the stratified sampling approach also are cells that would not be specified as constraints.

Additional constraints are used to match certain portfolio parameters with those of the index. The effective duration of the portfolio is the key parameter that is constrained within a very narrow range of the effective duration of the index. In some instances, an upper and lower bound as narrow as plus or minus 0.025 years from the effective duration of the index may be specified. Other parameters include average coupon, maturity, and quality.

Some constraints are used to implement an index fund manager's concerns about diversification or about extensive exposure to certain sectors of the market. For example, holdings in each corporate security can be constrained to a certain percentage of the portfolio to minimize the index fund's exposure to a particular issuer. Similarly, holdings in a particular sector can be constrained to a certain percentage of the portfolio; for example, the market value weight of securities issued by money center banks may be limited to a small percentage of the portfolio to reflect an index fund manager's concern about the size of Latin American debt and real estate loans in the loan portfolios of U.S. money center banks.

Finally, non-negativity constraints are used to reflect that a portfolio cannot have a negative holding of a security (i.e., a short sale or sale of a security not held in the portfolio). It should be noted that constraints specifying a minimum size for each holding to preclude holdings that are too small (and therefore impractical and costly to trade) are not included in linear programming problems. Such constraints must specify a minimum bound for each holding only if the holding has been selected and has a positive par amount; if the holding is zero (i.e., the security was not selected by the model), the constraint should not be effective. Such constraints are no longer linear and cannot be incorporated into the model. However, the need for minimum holdings has prompted users of linear programming models either to adjust the size of holdings after the portfolio has been selected by the model, or to remove the securities with small holdings from the basket of selected securities and then re-run the model with the remaining selected securities.

The third component to be specified is the universe of securities from which the optimization model can select issues. This universe is critical to the worthiness of the portfolio selected by the optimization model; if the securities selected by the optimization model are not valued correctly, or cannot be found at or near prices indicated in the portfolio, the value of the results of the optimization model is significantly reduced.

In its roughest form, the universe may be comprised of all the securities in the index and may contain such basic information on each security as "bid" side prices, yield-to-maturity, nominal duration, and term-to-maturity. The limitations of such a universe are the accuracy of the pricing of the securities; the availability of particular securities in the secondary market; and the absence of data to account for the call, put, and sinking fund features of each security. Including reliable data on call, put, and sinking fund features that is needed to generate such measures as effective yield and effective modified duration is a significant improvement. However, the problems associated with the reliability of pricing of securities and their availability cannot be resolved as easily. Pricing problems have plagued all fixed income databases including those maintained by large dealers. Pricing thousands of securities (some of which may not have traded for years) on a regular basis by traders or by computer-driven matrices is prone to sometimes-considerable error. The availability of particular securities—even if priced accurately—also is problematic because, as mentioned earlier, many of the securities are held in very inactive or low-turnover portfolios.

Pricing and availability difficulties may be partially addressed by reducing the number of securities in the universe. For example, securities below a certain issue size or issued before a given issue date may be eliminated from the universe. Similarly, securities that are particularly illiquid, based on recent trading volume, also may be dropped. Ideally, the narrowed-down universe should be refined further by reflecting the "long" and "short" positions in the market through price adjustments that will render some securities more attractive than others. (A long position occurs when a dealer owns a particular security in inventory and may be interested in selling the security at a small price concession. A short position occurs when a dealer has sold a security that he does not own to a third party, and may, therefore, be interested in purchasing the security at a premium in order to deliver the securities to the third party.) To date, such additional refinements have not been incorporated into any database, partly because of the extensive resources required to do so and partly because of the reluctance of dealers to provide information on their long and short positions on a systematic basis.

The optimization approach based on linear programming offers three major advantages. First, this optimization approach is systematic and comprehensive. The optimization model can be run easily on a regular basis, using the same objective function and set of constraints. The model can ensure that all appropriate cells are filled and their characteristics matched. Furthermore, the methodology does not depend on an index fund manager's thorough review of multiple reports to avoid overweightings and underweightings in different sectors.

Second, the optimization approach searches through an entire universe of securities to select the optimal combination that will provide the highest yield and convexity for a given portfolio structure. A manual scanning of available securities by an index fund manager may not provide the same yield and convexity levels.

Finally, the optimization approach enables an investment advisor with little or no index fund management expertise and resources to acquire index fund management capabilities readily through access to such a model. For example, an investment advisor can depend on a dealer with access to such a model to establish and rebalance an index fund. Stratified sampling, on the other hand, requires the time, judgment, and experience of an index fund manager.

Still, while a skillful formulation of the optimization problem overcomes some of the shortcomings of stratified sampling, the optimization approach based on linear programming has its own disadvantages.

One major disadvantage of the optimization approach is the broad, sweeping impact of the objective function. If, for example, an objective function is specified so as to maximize effective yield, the model will seek to maximize the effective yield of every cell, irrespective of an index fund manager's preference to implement a yield tilt only for particular cells. An index fund manager may choose to maximize effective yield in some of the corporate cells while maximizing convexity in all the Treasury and Yankee cells. Such selective yield and convexity tilts are not possible in the optimization approach, but they can be implemented readily in stratified sampling.

A second important disadvantage of the optimization approach is the high correlation between the quality of the portfolio selected by the model and the quality of the database specified as the universe. As described earlier, most publicly-available fixed income databases do not have accurate data on call, put, and sinking fund features of particular securities; nor do they have reliable prices. Furthermore, when the prices are reliable, the availability of many of the securities in the secondary market at those prices is not at all certain. Of course, one recourse is to use as substitutes other available securities with similar characteristics; however, as an index fund manager starts to substitute securities and adjust prices to reflect the market valuation of securities, the manager is, in effect, moving away from a true optimization approach toward stratified sampling.

Another recourse is to work with dealers who offer smaller databases (that only contain their own inventories or the securities they believe are available in the secondary market) in order to circumvent this pricing and availability problem. The key disadvantage of such databases is the requisite reliance on one dealer who offers only house inventory, or securities that can be located and re-sold at a profit. Securities available through another dealer at lower prices are, therefore, excluded from the portfolio.

In addition to the accuracy and reliability of data, most fixed income databases pose another problem for the optimization approach. The databases do not include several important sectors of the fixed income market, notably derivative and synthetic securities (including CMOs), STRIPS, medium-term note corporate bonds, and certificate of deposit notes issued by banks. Therefore, such securities would not be selected for an index fund using the optimization approach regardless of their potential value. In stratified sampling, on the other hand, the index fund manager readily can invest in such securities when establishing and rebalancing an index fund.

One of the disadvantages of the optimization approach is that the model cannot incorporate an index fund manager's preference for, and aversion to, particular corporate bond issuers. An index fund manager may prefer one of two available securities with similar prices and characteristics because the preferred security's credit rating is expected to be upgraded. The optimization model will not necessarily choose the preferred security. Conversely, one security may be considerably cheaper than another similar security and, therefore, be selected by the optimization model. The index fund manager, however, may not want that particular security because the issuer may become the target of a corporate takeover and become prone to deterioration in credit quality. But then if the index fund manager replaces securities selected by the optimization model, the manager is moving away from a true optimization toward stratified sampling.

Finally, optimization does not lend itself to partial rebalancing of an index fund and to security swaps as readily as stratified sampling. In a true optimization, an index fund manager cannot rebalance a particular sector of the index fund and ignore other sectors. For example, if the mortgage-backed securities held in an index fund experience high prepayments, the additional cash generated by the mortgage-backed sector can be reinvested only by re-optimizing and rebalancing the entire portfolio. Similarly, if an index fund manager takes advantage of attractive swaps in the secondary market and trades some securities for others, a true optimization approach would require that the entire portfolio be re-optimized and rebalanced in case the newly acquired securities impact the relative value of other securities held in the index fund. If such re-optimization is not performed, the index fund manager again is moving toward stratified sampling.

Optimization Approach Using Quadratic Programming

A third approach to indexing which shares some of the merits and pitfalls of the optimization approach using linear programming is the optimization approach using quadratic programming. Also known as variance minimization, this approach is the most complex of the three methodologies. In variance minimization, the objective is to select a basket of securities that will maximize expected return of the portfolio while minimizing the difference between the expected total return of the portfolio and that of its benchmark.

The variance minimization problem consists of three components: an objective function, a set of constraints and an opportunity set. However, unlike linear programming, the objective function plays a far more significant role than constraints do in determining the structure of the portfolio. Furthermore, the objective function is of quadratic rather than linear form. In variance minimization, the objective function maximizes utility where utility is defined as the difference between the expected return of an index fund and the risk of the index fund. Thus,

Utility = expected return on index fund – risk of index fund

where risk, or tracking error, is defined as the predicted standard deviation of the difference between the expected return of the index fund and the expected return of the index.

In this approach, an index fund manager determines the optimal trade-off between higher expected return and lower risk by specifying a risk aversion factor. A low risk aversion factor reduces the importance of tracking the returns of a benchmark for the benefit of higher expected return; a high risk aversion factor trades off portfolio return for greater tracking of the returns of the benchmark. The objective function that is maximized, therefore, can be restated as follows:

$$\text{Utility} = R_P - \lambda\,(V_P)$$

where

R_p is the expected excess return on the index fund,
λ is the risk aversion factor,
V_p is the variance of expected excess return on the index fund versus the index.

In indexing, the risk aversion factor is typically very large such that maximizing utility becomes equivalent to minimizing the variance of expected excess return (hence the name variance minimization). What determines expected return and variance of expected excess return?

The linchpin of the variance minimization approach is a risk factor model[2] which determines both the expected return of the index portfolio as well as the variance of expected excess return. Risk factor models consist of, among other things, a valuation model for pricing each bond in the opportunity set. Every bond is valued based on its exposure to two types of factors: (1) interest rates and interest-rate-related factors described as term structure factors; and (2) characteristics factors such as market sector, credit quality, coupon level, issue size, and call exposure.

The price of each bond is determined by discounting its cash flows according to its exposure to the different factors:

2. Much of the development of fixed income risk factor models was undertaken by BARRA, a fixed income and equity consulting and software firm in California. The description of risk factor models draws on BARRA's unpublished reports on the firm's Fixed Income Risk Model.

$$PV = \sum_{i=0}^{N} \frac{c_i r_i}{(1 + \sum_{j=1}^{J} x_j a_j)}$$

where

PV is the present value or the full price of the bond,

c_i is the cash flow at time i (a coupon payment or a coupon payment plus redemption value),

r_i is the discount factor at time i given the market term structure,

N is the number of periods until maturity,

X_j is the value of the bond's exposure to a characteristic factor,

a_j is the market's valuation of, or the yield spread attributed to, a characteristic factor,

J is the total number of characteristic factors.

The number of characteristic factors, J, varies in different risk factor models, and depends on the extent to which the model has been fine-tuned. For example, each bond's exposure to the corporate market sector may be described by one of four factors, namely an industrial, utility, finance or transportation factor; or, alternatively, the bond's exposure may be described by one of several factors in which each corporate sector is divided into subsectors and a factor descibes each subsector. The utility sector factor, for example, may be substituted by an electric, telephone, or natural gas transmission factor. Similarly, each bond's exposure to credit quality may be described either by one of four factors: AAA, AA, A and BBB, or by one of several factors in which each credit rating is divided into sub-categories and each sub-category credit rating includes ratings by Standard and Poor's and Moody's Investor Services—the two largest credit rating agencies. Typically, a risk factor model contains between 60 and 80 discount and characteristic factors; the number of discount factors for each bond depends on the number of years-to-maturity, and the number of characteristic factors depends on the type of security. Usually, most bonds are exposed to approximately five characteristic factors. When a bond is not exposed to a particular characteristic factor, i.e., factor j, the x_j of the bond for that factor is zero.

Given a bond valuation equation (as described above) for every bond in the opportunity set as well as reliable market prices for as many bonds as possible, an estimation procedure is used to determine the value for the discount and characteristic factors. This procedure is repeated over time to compile a history of the values for discount and characteristic factors. The historical data then is used to determine the two key components of a risk factor model: a covariance matrix that captures the correlation between discount factors and characteristic factors; and the variance of the discount and the characteristic factors. The covariance matrix measures, among other things, how the yield curve twists over time; the variance component measures how the two types of factors change over time. Once the covariance matrix, the variance of the factors, and the value of each bond have been estimated, the risk factor model generates a distribution of returns for every bond in the opportunity set. The distribution of expected returns for an index then is derived by a market-value weighting of the distribution of expected returns for all the bonds in the index.

At this point, the optimization model proceeds to select a basket of securities in which the distribution of expected returns will match the distribution of expected returns for an index, thereby minimizing tracking error. In effect, the optimization model selects a basket of securities whose risk exposure to the discount and characteristic factors matches that of the index.

In variance minimization, a set of constraints is specified also. However, most of the constraints are generic and apply to all optimizations regardless of the selected index. The constraints include a budget or cash constraint (that requires the sum of the weightings of each security to equal one), and lower and upper bound constraints (that prohibit short sales and excessively large holdings of particular issues).

Recently, users of the variance minimization approach have included additional constraints that are common to the linear programming approach. The constraints are designed so that the key parameters of the selected portfolio—notably duration, convexity, yield, and market sector exposure—match those of the index.

The opportunity set is the third component specified. Similar to linear programming, the opportunity set defines the universe from which securities are selected. Also similar to linear programming, variance minimization shares pitfalls relating to the pricing and reliability of data on securities in the opportunity set.

The most important advantage of variance minimization over linear programming and stratified sampling approaches to indexing is the use of the variance–covariance matrix. Discount factors and characteristic factors are correlated, and variance minimization is the only approach that exploits this correlation in selecting a basket of securities. If two securities are highly correlated (yet fall into different cells in the stratified sampling approach) and satisfy different constraints in the linear programming approach, the linear programming and stratified sampling methodologies may select both securities. Variance minimization, on the other hand, is less likely to select two highly correlated securities; it is more likely to choose a second security that will diversify issue-specific risk in the index fund.

Another advantage of variance minimization is the ability to measure the contribution to tracking error of each selected security. An index fund manager can examine and evaluate the role each security is expected to play in minimizing tracking error, and trade off the low contribution to tracking error of some selected securities for attractive features in other available securities. Of course, while securities can be substituted, it is important to note that the integrity of the initial optimal portfolio is violated; in fact, as more securities are substituted, the index fund manager moves increasingly away from variance minimization.

Variance minimization does have its shortcomings. One important shortcoming is the dependence of the risk factor model on historical data. The covariance matrix, and the variance of the discount and characteristic factors, are based on historical estimates for those factors. Often, more recent data is assigned a greater weighting than older data. Nevertheless, given the volatility and dynamic structure of the fixed income market, historical estimates are not always good indicators of the future behavior of discount and characteristic factors. Therefore, the basket of securities selected by the optimization model will be a portfolio with the lowest tracking error only if the pattern of past behavior of discount and characteristic factors, and their past correlation, continue in the future.

A second problem associated with variance minimization is the accuracy of the bond valuation model when data for particular characteristic factors is limited. When the market's valuation of a characteristic factor, i.e., the a_j, has been derived from a handful of securities, the estimate for the market's valuation may not be reliable. For example, historical data on securities that have an A+ credit rating from Standard and Poor's and an Aa2 credit rating from Moody's Investor Services is limited because only a handful of securities qualify for that particular combination of credit ratings. Therefore, the estimations for the market valuation of those split-rated issues may be erroneous.

Finally, while the complexities of variance minimization, and its bond valuation and risk factor model, can be explained, the reasoning for the selection of individual securities by the optimization model in a specific index fund is somewhat obscure. In stratified sampling, securities are selected because they fall into a particular cell and are cheaper (or have certain attributes that make them more attractive) than alternative securities that also fall into the same cell. Similarly in the linear programming approach, if the objective function maximizes yield, securities are selected because they meet all the constraints while having the highest yield. In variance minimization, however, an intricate pattern of variances and covariances determine which security is selected. While the value of the variances and covariances for each selected security can be examined, the selection of one security over another is a function of many relationships which an index fund manager cannot readily identify and isolate. Given such complexity, the ability of an index fund manager to measure the full implications of swapping securities in the index fund is limited to evaluating each security's contribution to tracking error.

Selecting the Appropriate Methodology

Selecting the most suitable of the three key approaches to indexing is a function of the type of index, the size of the index fund, the expertise of the index fund manager, the resources and analytical systems available to the index fund manager, and the type of index fund management.

If an index is simple and excludes securities with embedded options—callable and puttable corporate bonds and mortgage-backed securities—the three approaches are equally suitable, and will result in similar total returns in the long run. However if the index is more complex and includes securities such as mortgage-backed securities, stratified sampling and linear programming are more appropriate than variance minimization. While modeling the behavior of mortgage-backed securities has progressed considerably in recent years, and while the ability to evaluate securities with uncertain and wildly-variable cash flows has improved, estimates of the parameters of such securities still vary significantly among models. Given the dispersion of the estimates, it is inappropriate to use variance minimization to attribute an artificially high degree of certainty to those estimates. Instead, stratified sampling or linear programming may be used to construct an index fund that is diversified among coupon levels, types of securities, types of issuers and age of securities.

The size of an index fund also affects the suitability of each methodology. Stratified sampling and linear programming are more appropriate for large and medium-size index funds with assets over, say, $100 million. In such instances, the index—and consequently the index fund—can be divided into many cells; the investments in each can be diversified while maintaining tradeable and manageable lot sizes in each security. Smaller index funds cannot be divided into many cells because the dollar investments in each cell would be small and the number of holdings would be limited. Moreover, holdings that are a larger proportion of an index fund increase the level of non-systematic or issue-specific risk, thereby increasing the index fund's tracking error. Through exploiting the correlation among securities, variance minimization, on the other hand, allows for fewer holdings while maintaining the return profile of a diversified portfolio.

The expertise of an index fund manager and the extent of available resources and analytical systems, more than any other factor determine the suitability of each of the above methodologies. The two optimization approaches are more suitable for an index fund manager with little experience in managing index funds and in controlling the risk parameters of an index fund relative to an index. Limited working knowledge of the detailed structure of market indexes or of portfolio review systems that compare index funds to corresponding indexes can result in inadvertent biases in the index fund. Similarly, limited resources to continuously monitor and evaluate the index fund can leave such biases undetected for a long time. Under these circumstances, setting up and maintaining an index fund requires working with one of the financial services firms, all of whom use one of the optimization approaches. In addition, in stratified sampling, the selection of individual securities to fill the cells of an index fund requires both judgment and information on issues such as creditworthiness, relative value, call or prepayment exposure, and historical valuation. Providing such information to an index fund manager on a timely basis requires extensive resources.

Finally, consideration should be given to the type of index fund management. In an actively-managed index fund such as an enhanced fund with high turnover of securities, an optimization approach cannot be used to evaluate every trade or to restructure and reoptimize the portfolio after every trade. First, too much time is required to run either of the optimization models and then to fine-tune the results. Second, the opportunity sets used by the optimizations cannot capture the short-lived pricing inefficiencies and aberrations that can occur during the course of a given day. Third, running such optimizations can be expensive in terms of computer usage. Fourth, an index fund manager may select a security in anticipation of changes in future market valuations; optimizations, on the other hand, cannot select securities based on anticipated valuations. Therefore, a stratified sampling approach for the day-to-day management of index funds is more suitable.

Of course, one alternative is to use a combination of the indexing methodologies. Stratified sampling, for example, can be used for the daily active management of the index funds while linear programming or variance minimization can be used for a more comprehensive monitoring and possible restructuring of the index funds.

In fact, index fund managers often use analytical tools developed primarily for one indexing methodology in conjunction with another methodology. Cash flow structure analysis, also known as cash flow sculpturing, is one such tool. The purpose of cash flow structure analysis is to control the interest rate risk exposure of an index fund; interest rate risk exists when an index fund's expected return in response to parallel and non-parallel changes in the term structure of rates does not match that of an index fund. The risk is attributed to differences in duration and in the maturity distribution of securities between the index fund and the index; the source of the differences can be identified by cash flow structure analysis.

Exhibit 3-7 provides an example of such analysis. Specifically, the analysis compares the percentage of the present value of the index fund generated from coupon and principal payments at given intervals over the next 40 years to the percentage of the present value of the index at the same intervals. The frequency of the intervals can vary as shown in the first column of the exhibit. The share of the present value of the index fund and the index at each interval is shown in the second and third columns, respectively. The difference in the share of the present values, shown in the fourth column, explains the differences in interest rate exposure. A positive number, such as the 14.19 percent in the second interval, indicates an overweighting in the index fund. Conversely, a negative number, such as the negative 7.02 percent in the sixth interval, indicates an underweighting. A cash flow structure analysis of a portfolio with a barbell maturity structure relative to its index will have positive numbers in the early and the latter intervals, and negative numbers in the middle intervals.

While cash flow structure analysis was used initially in the variance minimization approach, it now also is used in the stratified sampling and linear programming approaches to control and monitor interest rate risk exposure.

Exhibit 3-7. Cash Flow Structure Analysis

Time	*Percent Of Present Value Allocated To Each Vertex For*		*Active*
	Portfolio	*Benchmark*	*Exposure*
.00	8.03%	2.23%	5.80%
.25	18.53	4.34	14.19
.50	1.64	2.85	-1.20
.75	3.74	2.34	1.40
1.00	2.96	7.64	-4.68
1.50	4.58	11.60	-7.02
2.00	3.39	8.98	-5.58
2.50	3.71	7.20	-3.49
3.00	3.37	5.97	-2.60
3.50	2.47	5.20	-2.73
4.00	3.91	6.74	-2.83
5.00	5.72	6.83	-1.11
6.00	5.54	5.39	0.14
7.00	9.22	9.44	-0.21
11.00	8.61	6.48	2.13
15.00	6.61	3.51	3.10
20.00	6.04	1.92	4.12
25.00	1.99	0.99	1.00
30.00	0.41	0.52	-0.11
35.00	0.10	0.02	0.08
40.00	0.00	0.01	-0.01

Source: BARRA

Rebalancing and Maintaining An Index Fund

Passive and actively-managed index funds must be rebalanced on a continuous basis. Several factors—some expected and others unexpected—account for the required rebalancing. The cash flow generated by an index fund, for example, must be reinvested. Cash flow includes interest payments, redemptions due to exercised call or put options or sinking fund programs, and principal payments in mortgage-backed securities. Occasional rebalancing also is required as securities age and have less than one year remaining to maturity; these securities are removed from an index and typically are removed from the index funds as well. Changes in the credit quality of the index fund in response to upgrading or downgrading of the credit rating of securities, and changes in sector weightings as different market sectors experience different total return, also can result in index fund imbalances. Another important factor that leads to index fund rebalancing is the change in the structure of the index itself; changes occur as new securities are added and others are removed, and as different interest-rate volatility and mortgage prepayment assumptions are specified.

Index funds can be rebalanced continuously or on a monthly basis. The frequency of rebalancing depends on the size and timing of the cash flows generated, on the type of changes in the index and the index fund, and of course, on whether the index fund is passively or actively managed. Unexpectedly large cash flows in the middle of the month reduce the duration of the index fund below that of the index. In such instances, reinvesting cash flows as they are received is less risky than rebalancing the entire portfolio at the end of the month. Similarly, an actively managed index fund is rebalanced continuously as securities are swapped and the characteristics of the index fund are changed.

Chapter 4

Realized Tracking Error

Realized tracking error is the difference between the total return of an index fund and that of a selected index, where the total return may be measured monthly, quarterly, or annually. If an index fund could invest proportionally in all securities contained in a selected index, its total return would match exactly that of the index and the realized tracking error would be zero. However, as noted in Chapter 4, index funds are limited to purchasing only a representative basket of securities whose characteristics and expected return match those of an index. Using such a basket of securities to represent an index inevitably leads to realized tracking error in both "pure" and enhanced index funds.

Realized tracking error is a performance evaluation tool for index fund investors, financial consultants, and index fund advisors. Indeed, index fund investors and financial consultants often use the magnitude and frequency distribution of realized tracking error to evaluate and select index fund advisors. In turn, index fund advisors examine realized tracking error to isolate any mismatches between the characteristics of their funds and those of the selected indexes.

This chapter first presents data on the magnitude of realized tracking error and then discusses five key factors that account for realized tracking error. The chapter concludes with a review of recent trends in using realized tracking error.

Magnitude of Realized Tracking Error

The magnitude of realized tracking error in an index fund depends primarily on the type and size of the index fund. Treasury and agency index funds have less realized tracking error than do corporate and mortgage-backed securities index funds because Treasury and agency securities have lower transaction costs and are more homogeneous. Similarly, large index funds (those with assets of $100 million or more) have less realized tracking error than do smaller index funds because the former can diversify non-systematic risk by holding more securities.

The magnitude of realized tracking error also depends on volatility of interest rates and of yield spreads. Risk characteristics of portfolios change in periods of high interest rate volatility. For example, the value of embedded options in corporate and mortgage-backed securities increases and option-adjusted durations shift either up or down. Such changes in risk characteristics occur in both index funds and in the corresponding benchmarks. As long as changes in an index fund match those of its benchmark, high interest rate volatility does not affect realized tracking error. Typically, however, since high volatility has a different impact on the risk characteristics of an index fund, an index fund has to be rebalanced more frequently to realign the fund's risk characteristics with its benchmark. The interim mismatches—and the transaction costs required to eliminate those mismatches—contribute to greater realized tracking error. Such mismatches are less likely in stable interest rate environments.

Similarly, realized tracking error increases in periods with high volatility of yield spread between the Treasury sector and other market sectors. If the sector weightings of an index fund do not match those of its benchmark exactly, a substantial change in yield spreads will have a different impact on the total return of an index fund than on that of the benchmark. For example, an index fund with the same option-adjusted yield as its benchmark may be underweighted in the agency sector and overweighted in the corporate sector. If yield spreads between the Treasury sector and the corporate sector widen, the index fund's total return will lag the return of the benchmark and realized tracking error will increase. Such a mismatch in sector weightings will not affect realized tracking error if yield spreads are stable.

In any discussion of realized tracking error, it is important to specify the horizon over which realized tracking error has been measured. Realized tracking error can be measured over any horizon for which total return data on both an index fund and its corresponding benchmark is available. Typically, realized tracking error is measured over monthly, quarterly, and annual periods. Monthly and quarterly data are used to monitor the extent to which an index fund advisor deviates from a selected benchmark. Volatile monthly realized tracking error, for example, may signify unintended biases or unsuccessful strategies in the index fund. Annual data—or annualized for periods spanning more than one year—are used to evaluate the investment expertise of an index fund advisor. For example, low realized tracking error in a pure index fund may signify a well-diversified portfolio correctly matched to an index fund; large positive annual realized tracking error in an enhanced index fund, on the other hand, may be attributed to the value added by the index fund advisor.

What has been the magnitude of reported realized tracking error? With the exception of a handful of billion dollar-plus index funds with annual realized tracking error under five basis points, most broad market index funds with assets over $100 million have experienced annual realized tracking error of between five and 20 basis points. In smaller broad market index funds of under $100 million, annual realized tracking error of 20 to 30 basis points is not uncommon. Finally, in a large Treasury and agency index fund, annual realized tracking error of zero to five basis points can be expected because the index fund can invest in most—if not all—of the Treasury securities contained in the index (which together represent 85 percent of a Treasury and agency index).

Exhibit 4-1 summarizes the result of a detailed Salomon Brothers Inc. study[1] on realized tracking error. The study simulated the

---

1. "Broad Investment-Grade Bond Index: Index Replication Analysis", January 1986, and a tracking error report prepared for the author.

Exhibit 4-1. Tracking Error of Monthy Returns in Basis Points (1984-1985)

($100 million Index Fund)

	Range			*Mean*			
				Absolute	*Standard*		
Sector	*High*	*Low*	*Mean*	*Deviation*	*Deviation*	*Cumulative*	*Annualized*
Broad Market	13	–6	2	4	5	69	34
Governments	5	–1	2	2	2	63	31
Corporates*	40	–26	9	16	17	301	156
Mortgages	6	–7	0	2	3	6	3
Broad Market (including transaction costs)	11	–8	0	4	5	–12	–6

*Tracking error for corporates measured between January 1985 and November 1986.

Source: Salomon Brothers Inc., based on Salomon Brothers Broad Investment-Grade Bond Index and its components.

returns of $50 million and $100 million index funds designed to track the Salomon Brothers Inc.'s indexes over a two-year period. Salomon Brothers Inc.'s index optimization system based on linear programming was used to select securities; the index funds were rebalanced monthly.

Returns for two types of index funds were simulated: (1) broad market index funds designed to track the entire Salomon Brothers BIG Index, and (2) market sector index funds designed to track a specific component of the Salomon Brothers BIG Index. The three market sector index funds examined in this chapter are based on the government, corporate, and mortgage-backed securities component of the Salomon Brothers BIG Index. It is important to note that the realized tracking error of a market sector index fund, say, a mortgage-backed securities fund designed to track the mortgage-backed securities components of the Salomon Brothers BIG Index, is lower than the realized tracking error in mortgage-backed securities holdings of a broad market index fund designed to track the entire index.

Several statistics are used to measure the magnitude of realized tracking error. The most widely used measures are the average—or mean—realized tracking error of monthly or quarterly data, and the annualized realized tracking error for periods of one or more years. The statistics in Exhibit 4-1 are based on the monthly tracking error over a two-year period.

Mean and annualized tracking error provide little information about the dispersion of realized tracking error. Such information is contained in the mean absolute deviation (the average of the absolute value of the monthly or quarterly realized tracking error), standard deviation, and range of monthly or quarterly realized tracking error. The mean absolute deviation is a more useful measure of the magnitude of realized tracking error because it accounts for the latter's positive or negative direction. For example, realized tracking error of 10 basis points in one month followed by a realized tracking error of negative 10 basis points in the subsequent month will result in a mean realized tracking error of zero basis points. The mean absolute deviation, however, will stand at 10 basis points which, compared to the mean, better represents the magnitude of realized tracking error that can be expected in any given period. The standard deviation conveys information on the probability of encountering different magnitudes of realized tracking error in any given period; this measure assumes realized tracking error is normally distributed. Finally, the range of realized tracking error provides information on the highest and lowest monthly or quarterly realized tracking error.

In the Salomon Brothers Inc. study, the index fund designed to track the corporate component of the Salomon Brothers BIG Index exhibited the greatest realized tracking error (Exhibit 4-1). At nine basis points, the average realized monthly tracking error of the corporate index fund was more than four times greater than that of other specific sector and broad market index funds. The mean absolute deviation of 16 basis points and the standard deviation of 17 basis points were more than three times greater than those of all other index funds. The highest positive monthly realized tracking error stood at 40 basis points and the highest negative monthly realized tracking error stood at 26 basis points, compared with the next highest positive realized tracking error for a particular sector of six basis points (mortgages) and the next highest negative realized tracking error of minus seven basis points (also mortgages). Volatile realized tracking error in the corporate sector occurs frequently; because of their limited size, most index funds cannot eliminate all the non-systematic risk of corporate securities. Event risk and, to a lesser extent, call risk are examples of such non-systematic risk. Illiquidity (and therefore unreliable pricing) and the higher transaction costs of corporate securities also contribute to volatile realized tracking error.

Despite such volatile realized tracking error, the corporate index fund outperformed its benchmark by 301 basis points over the 23-month period. This magnitude of outperformance in a corporate index fund is unusually high and should be attributed to the optimization system used by Salomon Brothers Inc. The system's selection of individual corporate securities—maximizing yield and minimizing call exposure (particularly in periods like 1985 and 1986)—account for most of the outperformance.

Based on monthly realized tracking error and its dispersion, the government sector had the lowest realized tracking error; the highest positive realized tracking error was five basis points and the highest negative realized tracking error stood at minus one; the mean, the mean absolute deviation, and the standard deviation were two basis points each. Realized tracking error in a government index fund is attributed to differences in total return between current coupon (most recently auctioned or on-the-run) and off-the-run Treasury securities, changes in the relative value of Treasury securities, different reinvestment income between the index fund and its benchmark, and transaction costs.

Based on cumulative realized tracking error, however, the mortgage-backed securities index fund had the lowest realized tracking error. The index fund outperformed the two-year total return of its benchmark by only six basis points, compared to 63 basis points for the government index fund. This data, however, should be viewed with caution; matching the returns of a mortgage-backed securities index while maintaining low monthly and annualized realized tracking error is more difficult than indicated by the data.

In this simulation, two sources of realized tracking error in the mortgage sector were eliminated. First, aggregated prepayment data on all mortgage pools in the mortgage component of the Salomon Brothers BIG Index was used to measure the returns of the mortgage index fund. Therefore, the prepayment rates and, consequently, the principal and income returns for each type of mortgage-backed security with a given coupon level and age in the index fund matched those of the mortgage benchmark. In practice, such an exact match does not occur. Second, the prices used for measuring returns of the index fund were aggregated for each type of mortgage-backed security with a given coupon level and age, and matched the prices used for the mortgage benchmark. In practice, many mortgage pools including seasoned FNMA and FHLMC pools are priced individually rather than in unison with all other mortgage pools securitized by the same agency with the same coupon level and age. And, the individual prices will not match the aggregated prices of the mortgage benchmark.

Finally, realized tracking error for the index fund designed to match the returns of the Salomon Brothers BIG Index fell between the extreme volatility of the corporate index fund and the relative stability of the government and mortgage-backed securities index funds with a mean, mean absolute deviation, and standard deviation of two, four, and five basis points, respectively. The two-year cumulative realized tracking error of 69 basis points closely matched the 63-basis-point realized tracking error of the government index fund, reflecting the 55 percent weighting of government securities in the broad market benchmark.

The study also measured the impact of transaction costs on realized tracking error. Annualized realized tracking error for the broad market index fund was reduced from a positive 34 basis points to a negative six points, and the mean was reduced from two to zero basis points. Transaction costs, therefore, reduced the performance of the simulated index fund by 40 basis points.

Smaller asset size had a negative impact on realized tracking error as well. As shown in Exhibit 4-2, a $50 million broad market index fund exhibited nearly 50 percent greater realized tracking error than did a $100 million index fund. The highest positive monthly realized tracking error stood at 22 basis points (13 basis points for the larger index fund); the highest negative monthly tracking error stood at 10 basis points (minus six basis points for the larger index fund). The mean absolute deviation and the standard deviation also were greater. Drag on performance incurred by smaller index funds is seen in the annualized positive tracking error of 28 basis points, compared with 34 basis points for $100 million index fund. Finally, as with the large index fund, transaction costs reduced the performance of the small index fund by nearly 40 basis points.

Sources of Realized Tracking Error

Realized tracking error of pure index funds is attributable to five factors: non-systematic or issue-specific risk; price differentials; transaction costs; imprecise and variable estimates of key index and

Exhibit 4-2. Tracking Error of Monthly Returns in Basis Points (1984-1985)

($50 million Index Fund)

Sector	*Range*		*Mean*	*Mean Absolute Deviation*	*Standard Deviation*	*Cumulative*	*Annualized*
	High	*Low*					
Broad Market	22	–10	2	6	8	56	28
Broad Market (including trans-action costs)	19	–13	–1	7	8	–20	–10

Source: Salomon Brothers Inc., based on Salomon Brothers Broad Investment-Grade Bond Index.

index fund characteristics; and theoretical and sometimes impractical assumptions used in calculating index returns. The impact of these factors can be reduced, and varies with type and size of index funds; however, with the exception of billion dollar-plus index funds, realized tracking error cannot be totally eliminated.

Non-systematic or issue-specific risk is a source of realized tracking error whose impact is significantly reduced in large index funds as well as in Treasury and agency index funds. Non-systematic risk is the risk associated with owning a limited number of securities in a portfolio; total return of any portfolio is explained partly by the total return of a market index and partly by the unique features of individual securities in that portfolio. A large bond portfolio composed of many different securities can have low non-systematic risk when the unique features of any particular security have a small impact on the returns of the entire portfolio. In such a case, most of the portfolio's return is explained by the return of the market index. A small portfolio cannot be as well diversified, therefore the non-systematic component of total returns can be significant.

A market index, by definition, has zero non-systematic risk. A market index, such as the Salomon Brothers BIG Index or the Lehman Brothers Aggregate Index, contains over four thousand corporate securities and also represents over 300 thousand specific mortgage pools. Broad market index funds, in contrast, have positive non-systematic risk because they include only a limited number of securities to represent the market indexes containing thousands of securities. Non-systematic risk is greatest in the corporate and mortgage-backed securities components of index funds.

In the corporate market, unanticipated changes in credit quality, in marketability, and in call (or put) exposure account for non-systematic risk. In recent years, the single largest source of non-systematic risk has been the restructuring of corporations due to mergers, acquisitions and leveraged buy-outs. This type of non-systematic risk, also called event risk, often has resulted in significant credit deterioration and price loss in the securities of restructured corporations. And the negative impact on the total return of an index fund with a limited number of securities is magnified relative to the impact on the total return of an index. The price loss of nearly 15 percent in some RJR Nabisco Inc. bonds following the takeover of the company in December 1988 exemplifies the exposure of index funds to non-systematic risk. At the time, RJR Nabisco Inc. accounted for less than 0.15 percent of the market value of the Salomon Brothers BIG Index, but the issuer most likely represented a larger percentage of many existing index funds.

In the mortgage market, non-systematic risk exists because of the wide range of prepayment rates among pools within each coupon and type of mortgage-backed security. In an index, each coupon and type of mortgage-backed security is represented by one generic issue. The generic issue is an aggregation of all outstanding mortgage-backed pools—several thousand in some instances—that have the same coupon and type of issuer[2] (i.e., Ginnie Mae, Fannie Mae, or Freddie Mac). An index fund, however, can invest in only a limited number of pools in its effort to replicate the generic issue. Since the prepayment rates of the selected pools may not match those of the generic issue, the total return of the selected pools may diverge from that of the generic issue in the index.

Exhibit 4-3 illustrates the impact of different prepayment rates on total return. Two generic cases each are compared with a faster and a slower pool: a Ginnie Mae Single Family 30-year mortgage-backed security with a 12 percent coupon; and a Freddie Mac Conventional Guarantor Single Family 30-year seasoned mortgage-backed security with a nine percent coupon. The generic issue in each example represents the aggregated data of all pools that have the same coupon, issuer and level of seasoning, and therefore represents the corresponding mortgage-backed security in a market index.

In the first case, the generic issue represents the aggregated data of over 8,000 Ginnie Mae Single Family 30-year pools and accounts for 1.5 percent of the market value of mortgage indexes. The generic issue has had a constant prepayment rate (CPR) of 23 percent for the 12-month period ending November 1988.[3] At this CPR

2. Some market indexes aggregate pools based on their coupon, type of issue, as well as their age (also referred to as seasoning).

3. Period selected to show wide range of prepayment rates.

Exhibit 4-3. Non-systematic Risk in Mortgage-Backed Securities

Type	*Coupon*	*Pool*	*12-Month CPR**	*1-Year Total Return (unchanged market)*	*Return Difference (from generic)*
GNMA	12.00%	Generic	23%	9.37%	0%
GNMA	12.00	124439	36%	8.28	−1.09
GNMA	12.00	58317	0%	11.23	1.86
FHLMC	9.00	Generic Seasoned	8%	10.05	0
FHLMC	9.00	251337	4%	9.85	−0.20
FHLMC	9.00	289879	13%	10.26	0.21

*Historical Constant Prepayment Rate for a 12-month period.

rate and in an unchanged interest rate environment, the generic issue produces a total return of about 9.37 percent in the mortgage index.

In the second case, the generic issue represents the aggregated data of about 1,300 Freddie Mac Conventional Guarantor Single Family 30-year pools that were issued prior to 1984. The generic issue has had a 12-month CPR of eight percent. At this CPR rate and in an unchanged interest rate environment, the generic issue produces a total return of about 10.05 percent in a mortgage index.

Unlike the total return of a mortgage index which is determined by the CPR of generic issues, the total return of a mortgage index fund is determined by the CPR of the particular pools in the portfolio. To represent the generic issues, a $100 million index fund may hold only one or two Ginnie Mae Single Family 30-year 12-percent pools and one or two seasoned Freddie Mac Conventional Guarantor Single Family 30-year nine percent pools. The prepayment rates of the particular pools probably will differ from the generic issues, thereby contributing to realized tracking error.

In the first case, if the 12-percent Ginnie Mae pools (purchased at a price above par in December 1989) have a CPR that is higher than that of the generic issue, the total return of the pools will lag that of the generic issue, which results in negative realized tracking error. Pool Number 124439, for example, with a CPR of 36 percent produces a total return of 8.28 percent, underperforming the generic issue by negative 1.09 percent. In contrast, Pool Number 58317 with a zero percent CPR produces a total return of 11.23 percent, outperforming the generic issue in the index by 1.86 percent, which contributes to positive realized tracking error.

In the case of the nine percent Freddie Macs (purchased at a price below par in December 1989), pools with slower prepayment rates than the generic issue contribute to negative realized tracking error. Pool Number 2511337, for example, with a CPR of four percent, will underperform the generic issue by 20 basis points; Pool Number 289879 with a CPR of 13 percent will outperform the generic issue by 21 basis points.

Therefore given the wide range of prepayments among pools of the same type, coupon level, and age, realized tracking error in the mortgage component of an index fund can be significant. In very large index funds, the magnitude of expected tracking error can be reduced by holding multiple pools to represent each generic issue. A larger number of pools should result in prepayment rates that match more closely the rates of each generic issue.

Non-systematic risk is not a major factor in Treasury and agency securities, both of which are more homogeneous than corporate and mortgage-backed securities.

Price differentials are another important source of realized tracking error. As noted in Chapter 3, fixed income securities do not trade in a centralized exchange from which uniform prices might be obtained. In fact, at any given time, different fixed income traders are willing to purchase (or sell) the same security at a different price. The magnitude of price differentials may be measured when a security is sold or purchased through a "competitive process;" in this process, an investment advisor obtains prices for a security from several dealers and executes a trade (purchase or sale) with the dealer providing the best price. The difference between the highest and lowest price can be significant, even if occasional outliers are excluded.

In Exhibit 4-4, bid prices from a competitive selling process are shown. The trades included the sale of a Treasury, an agency, a corporate and a mortgage-backed security. In these selected examples representing actual trades with some of the largest dealers in the country, the price differentials were unusually wide. Even in the more efficient and more liquid Treasury market, the price differential for the 10.375 percent coupon Treasury maturing on November 15, 2009 (and callable in 2004) between the highest and the lowest bidder was very wide at ten thirty-seconds. A price differential of four thirty-seconds in off-the-run Treasury securities is not uncommon.

The price differential of thirty thirty-seconds for the Federal Farm Credit Bank security was extremely wide as well, particularly given the relatively short maturity of the issue. The widest differential occurred, as expected, in the corporate market where the difference between the highest and the lowest bidder was \$3.062 per hundred. Price differential in the mortgage-backed security was the

Exhibit 4-4. Price Differentials

Market bids for actual trades

Dealer	*TSY 10.375% 11/15/09*	*FFCB 14.25 4/20/94**	*B.C. Hydro 15.5 7/15/11***	*GNSF 9.50****
A	110^{14}	123^{28}	133.25	96^{24} (L)
B	110^{21} (H)	124^{6}	131.726 (L)	96^{26}
C	110^{17}	124^{8} (H)	134.324	96^{28} (H)
D	110^{11} (L)	123^{18}	134.788 (H)	96^{25}
E	110^{21} (H)	123^{10} (L)	134.45	96^{28} (H)
Difference between highest and lowest price in percent	0.28%	0.76%	2.32%	0.13%

*Federal Farm Credit Bank
**British Columbia Hydro and Power
***Ginnie Mae Single Family 30-Year

Treasury, agency, and mortgage-backed securities quoted in 32nds.

narrowest at four thirty-seconds. Again, while the price differential examples selected for this exhibits are wider than usual, price differentials are sufficiently wide to affect realized tracking error.

Price differentials contribute to realized tracking error through general trading activity and through portfolio valuation. First, tracking error is realized when an index fund advisor trades a security with one dealer while the index is priced by another dealer. An index fund advisor, for example, would sell the Treasury 10.375s of November 15, 2009 to dealer B or Dealer E in Exhibit 4-4; securities in the index however, may be priced by, say, Dealer D. The price differential between Dealer B and Dealer D will contribute 0.28 percent of positive realized tracking error. In the case of the corporate bond, if the trade is executed with Dealer D while Dealer B is pricing the securities in the index, the contribution to realized tracking error is 2.32 percent. Of course, the impact on the realized tracking error of the entire index fund will depend on the market value share of the security relative to the index fund. Therefore, unless all trades are executed either with the dealer who is pricing the securities in the index or with other dealers at prices that match index prices, tracking error will be realized.

Second, price differentials contribute to realized tracking error by causing different month-end portfolio valuations. Portfolio accounting systems, custodial pricing services and producers of market indexes often have different valuations for the same index fund; consequently, monthly, quarterly and even annual total returns will differ, depending on the source of the index fund valuation. Realized tracking error is, therefore, inevitable when an index fund is not valued by the producer of the selected index.

It is important to note that the impact on realized tracking error of price differentials is minimized in large index funds with many securities because the positive price differential in one security is often offset by the negative price differential in another security. Furthermore, in the long run, differences in index fund valuations in one month (or quarter) are offset by differences in subsequent periods. For example, if a custodial pricing service overestimates the returns of an index fund in one period, the service is likely to underestimate the returns in a subsequent period. Such offsetting estimates can be observed in periods which end on days with high interest rate volatility. On volatile days, differences in index fund valuations can be attributed directly to differences in the time of day at which prices are recorded (e.g., 3:00 p.m. E.S.T. versus 5:00 p.m. E.S.T.). A significant market move after 3:00 p.m. E.S.T., for example, on the last day of the month will affect the returns of an index (or index fund) that is priced at 3:00 p.m. E.S.T. in the following month; an index (or index fund) that is priced at 5:00 p.m. E.S.T. will capture the market move in the same month that the move occurred.

Transaction costs are the third source of realized tracking error. An index fund incurs transaction costs—the spread between purchase price and sale price—when income as well as principal payments (from mortgage-backed securities and from securities that have matured or been called or put) are reinvested, securities are swapped, or the portfolio structure is rebalanced. Such trading activity results in the purchase of securities, all of which are acquired at the offer—or ask—side of the market. When purchased securities are valued in an index fund, however, they are marked down to the bid side of the market. As a result, the subsequent total returns of an index fund incorporate the negative impact of transaction costs.

Broad market index funds, on the other hand, do not account for the negative impact of transaction costs. Securities in all broad market indexes are priced at the bid side of the market and any reinvestment of income and principal—as well as turnover due to securities dropping out of, or being added to, the index—typically occur at the bid side.[4] Total return calculations of broad market indexes, therefore, ignore the negative impact of transaction costs (which are included in the total return of index funds). The difference in the treatment of transaction costs results in negative realized tracking error.

The magnitude of transaction costs can be measured by the bid-ask spread of individual securities. In Treasury, agency, and generic mortgage-backed securities, bid-ask spreads typically range from one to four thirty-seconds; in corporate and seasoned mortgage-backed securities and in some of the derivative instruments like asset-backed securities and collateralized mortgage obligations, bid-ask spreads typically range from four thirty-seconds to as much as one-half of one percent. Bid-ask spreads or some corporate securities have been as wide as five points.

It should be noted that the contribution of transaction costs to realized tracking error will depend on both the type of securities traded as well as on the level of turnover. In the Salomon Brothers Inc. study summarized earlier, portfolio turnover for the broad market $100 million index fund averaged 11 percent a month (Exhibit 4-5), and resulted in annualized transaction costs of 40 basis points. Portfolio turnover for the broad market $50 million index fund averaged 10 percent a month and resulted also in 40 basis points of annualized transaction costs.

---

4. In the Lehman Brothers Aggregate Index, new issue corporate securities are added to the Index at the offer side of the market. In the Salomon Brothers BIG Index, new issue Treasury, corporate, and mortgage-backed securities are added to the Index at the offer side.

Exhibit 4-5. Index Fund Monthly Turnover (1984-1985)*

$100 million Index Fund

Sector	*High*	*Low*	*Mean*
Broad Market	17.6%	4.3%	11.1%
Governments	16.7	3.7	8.9
Corporates	23.0	7.4	15.9
Mortgages	5.1	1.2	2.6

*Excludes initial turnover of 100% when portfolio is funded with cash. Based on purchase turnover. Corporate data is from January 1985 through November 1986.

Source: Salomon Brothers Inc., based on Salomon Brothers Broad Investment-Grade Bond Index and its components.

A fourth source of realized tracking error is the variability and imprecision of the measures of index and index fund risk and return characteristics. Characteristics such as effective modified duration also called option-adjusted or call-adjusted duration and convexity can only be estimated; furthermore, the estimates have a wide degree of dispersion.

Exhibit 4-6 compares five dealers' estimates of the effective duration and option-adjusted spread (as a proxy for convexity cost) of a Freddie Mac Conventional Guarantor 30-year mortgage-backed security with a 12 percent coupon. Dealer D estimated an effective duration of 2.7 years while Dealer E, at 1.2 years, estimated an effective duration that was 56 percent lower. The two dealers also estimated very different convexity costs for the generic Freddie Mac. Such wide differences in risk and return estimates also are seen in other mortgage-backed, corporate, and, to a lesser extent, government securities with embedded options. Furthermore, the differences extend into the risk and return estimates of broad market indexes and subsectors of broad market indexes.

The dispersion in dealers' estimates—or the estimates of financial software organizations—readily can be attributed to differences in each dealer's volatility assumption, mortgage prepayment model, option model, and, for those dealers who have one, their model on

Exhibit 4-6. Range of Estimates of Effective Duration and Option-Adjusted Yield Spreads

	Freddie Mac Conventional Guarantor 30-Year 12%	
Dealer	*Effective Duration*	*Option-Adjusted Yield Spreads*
A	1.8 years	3 basis points
B	2.2	46
C	1.7	−12
D	2.7	69
E	1.2	−24
Range	1.5	93

corporate refunding patterns. However even if the source of the dispersion is determined, an index fund advisor still must identify and then match appropriate target durations and option-adjusted spreads in the index fund, and in subsectors and "cells" (see Chapter 3) in the index fund. Identifying appropriate target durations and option-adjusted spreads as well as matching those target levels can prove elusive, given the dispersion inherent in such risk and return estimates.

Moreover, an index fund advisor also must attempt to match the expected change in target durations and option-adjusted spreads of an index fund (in response to shifts in interest rates and interest rate volatility) to the expected change in target durations and option-adjusted spreads of the selected index, i.e., match the convexity of an index fund to that of the selected index. Otherwise in volatile interest rate environments, the initial match between the index fund and the index might unravel, total returns may differ, and the index fund may have to be restructured, all of which contribute to realized tracking error.

Finally, a fifth source—albeit a marginal source—of realized tracking error is the theoretical and sometimes impractical assumptions used in calculating index total returns. Calculating index total returns requires certain assumptions about reinvestment of income, discounting of cashflows, and level of accrued interest of mortgage-backed securities. In theory, some of the assumptions are accurate; in practice, these assumptions cannot be implemented when managing index funds. For example, in calculating the total return of the Salomon Brothers BIG Index, intra-month cashflows are reinvested as received in the daily average one-month Treasury bill rate for that month. In the Lehman Brothers Aggregate Index, coupon income is not invested until month-end, at which time the coupon income is reinvested into the index. In practice, however, index fund advisors are not able to always invest cashflows at the rates assumed in the Salomon Brothers BIG Index. And index fund advisors typically do not wait until month-end to reinvest the received cashflows.

Similarly, the assumptions about discounting cashflows from mortgage-backed securities to the end of a prior month in order to calculate monthly index returns do not reflect the actual receipt and reinvestment of cashflows from mortgage-backed securities. As discussed in Chapter 2, each broad market index is based on different technical assumptions regarding the intra-month settlement dates of mortgage-backed securities, and the reinvestment of principal and income received. Furthermore, broad market indexes calculate total return on the basis of accrued principal and income payments while most index funds' total returns are calculated on the basis of actual receipt of principal and income payments. Accrual rather than cash-basis accounting will contribute to realized tracking error only when prepayments change significantly from one month to the next.

Finally, the assumptions regarding the level of accrued interest in mortgage-backed securities at month-end differ from how index funds are valued at month-end by custodial services and by portfolio analysis systems. For example, the Salomon Brothers BIG Index total returns are based on a zero level of accrued interest for mortgage-backed securities; most index fund total returns are based on a portfolio value with one-month of accrued interest.

It should be noted that while these inaccurate or impractical assumptions contribute to realized tracking error, the magnitude of their contribution is negligible.

Using Realized Tracking Error

Realized tracking error is used increasingly by index fund investors and financial consultants to evaluate the performance of index fund advisors. Index fund investors and financial consultants now request quarterly performance data on index funds and on the corresponding benchmarks when selecting an index fund advisor. Quarterly data is necessary to measure consistency, thoroughness and degree of risk control of the index fund advisor. In some instances, large positive and negative quarterly realized tracking error over an extended period (in a pure $100 million index fund) may signify the lack of analytical systems that match the risk characteristics of an index fund to those of an index. In contrast, large realized tracking error in a particular market environment in an enhanced index fund (see Chapter 5) may reflect the strengths—or lack thereof—of an index fund advisor's investment style in that particular market environment. For example, focusing on issue selection in a market environment suited to sector selection may result in high turnover and negative realized tracking error while providing no incremental return over a given period.

More recently, index fund advisors have been requested to attribute realized tracking error to possible sources, including mismatches in risk characteristics of their index funds and specific investment strategies. Requests for proposals for managing index funds often require examples of successful and unsuccessful investment strategies as well as an evaluation of the strategies' contribution to realized tracking error.

Realized tracking error is a useful tool for index fund advisors as well. Identifying the sources of realized tracking error enables an index fund advisor to better control the risk characteristics of an index fund. After examining the realized tracking error of an index fund, an advisor should be able to attribute the realized tracking error to one or more of the five sources described earlier in the chapter. Any residual tracking error is due to either a specific investment strategy implemented by the index fund advisor or an inadvertent mismatch of risk characteristics between the index fund and its corresponding benchmark.

Chapter 5

Enhanced Indexing

Enhanced indexing or "index plus" is a form of index fund management that aims to outperform a particular index while matching its major risk characteristics. Two factors distinguish enhanced indexing from pure, or vanilla, indexing.

The first distinguishing factor is the degree of active management and, hence, of portfolio turnover. Pure index funds are passively-managed portfolios, in which trades are made only when necessary to rebalance the portfolio and to realign the portfolio's risk and return characteristics with those of the index. Enhanced index funds are actively-managed portfolios in which trades are intended to rebalance the portfolio and, additionally, to capture any available investment opportunities. Therefore, enhanced funds typically have higher turnover rates than pure index funds.

The second distinguishing factor is the direction and magnitude of realized tracking error. Pure index funds are managed with the objective of minimizing realized tracking error, while enhanced index funds are managed with the objective of maximizing positive realized tracking error. The magnitude of positive realized tracking error—the amount of potential enhancement—depends on four factors: (i) the type of index fund; (ii) the strategies employed by an index fund advisor; (iii) the latitude given to an index fund advisor to deviate from a selected index; and (iv) the level of volatility of interest rates and market sector spreads.

Type of index fund. Broad market index funds permit greater enhancement of total returns than do specialized market sector index funds. A specialized market sector index fund is restricted to one sector and, therefore, to investment opportunities in that sector only. A broad market index fund, on the other hand, can add value by allocating assets among different market sectors and by taking advantage of specific investment opportunities in each of those market sectors.

Strategies employed by an index fund advisor. The potential for enhancing total return is greatest if an index fund advisor takes advantage of multiple investment strategies including sector selection, yield curve strategies, coupon selection, issuer selection, and use of derivative and synthetic securities. Specialization in one type of strategy limits the degree of enhancement, particularly when the prevailing market environment does not favor that strategy.

The latitude given an index fund advisor. The greater the latitude to deviate from certain risk and return characteristics of the benchmark, the greater is the potential to enhance the returns of the index fund. Of course, greater latitude to deviate also means greater risk of underperforming the benchmark. An index fund will have large tracking error when both its sector weightings deviate significantly from those of the benchmark and fluctuations occur in yield spreads between the Treasury, corporate, and mortgage-backed securities markets.

The level of volatility of interest rates and market sector spreads. When volatility is low, mispricings of sectors and individual securities—and hence investment opportunities to enhance returns—are reduced. Conversely, when the volatility of both interest rates and of market sector spreads is high, an index fund advisor can enhance returns by taking advantage of inefficiencies in the relative value of securities, of changes in the shape of the yield curve and of fluctuations in yield spreads.

The type of index fund, the strategies employed, the latitude given and the level of volatility notwithstanding, an enhanced index fund is expected to provide at least 25 basis points of incremental value per year. Fifty basis points annually represents the average annual incremental return that is typically offered by enhanced index fund advisors. Occasionally, an enhanced index fund advisor may quote a multi-year target enhancement of as much as 100 basis points per year. To put this claim in perspective it should be cautioned that such a return would require a level of performance leading to top quartile ranking among all active fixed income advisors.

The rest of this chapter describes alternative investment strategies to enhance the returns of an index fund. Descriptions of key investment strategies is followed by a review of the trade-off between potential incremental return and the risk of underperformance. Similarities and differences between enhanced indexing and two active fixed income disciplines—notably risk- (or duration-) control and sector rotation—then are examined. Finally, the chapter concludes with a review of the advantages and disadvantages of enhanced indexing compared to pure indexing.

Five investment strategies are used to enhance the returns of an index fund. These strategies are implemented while maintaining the same effective duration as that of the benchmark; hence the strategies are sometimes called duration-neutral strategies. These strategies also are used by traditional active managers though often in combination with extending or shortening the portfolio's duration.

Market Sector Selection

The first investment strategy—and the strategy with the greatest impact on an index fund's potential to outperform or underperform a benchmark—is market sector selection. Market sector selection is the underweighting or overweighting of one or more market sectors in a given index. Broad market indexes such as the Salomon Brothers BIG Index, the Lehman Brothers Aggregate Bond Index or the Merrill Lynch Domestic Master Index, are comprised of four market sectors: the Treasury, agency, corporate and mortgage-backed securities sectors.

In more specialized indexes, broad market sectors give way to subsectors of the agency, corporate, and mortgage-backed securities markets. In an agency index, subsectors are delineated by the government agencies or quasi-agencies that issue securities contained in the index. Examples of such agencies are the Federal Farm Credit Bank (FFCB), the Federal Home Loan Bank Board (FHLBB), the Student Loan Marketing Association (SLMA), the Federal National Mortgage Association (FNMA), and the Financing Corporation (FICO). In a corporate index, subsectors are delineated by the type of issuer; the issuers include utilities, bank and finance companies, industrial companies, and Yankee issuers. Finally, in a mortgage-backed securities index, subsectors are delineated by the type of issue (Ginnie Mae, Fannie Mae, or Freddie Mac), the type of mortgage (30-year or 15-year), and the age of the security (new or seasoned).

The decision to overweight or underweight a given market sector or subsector is based on an index fund advisor's expectations of future yield spreads between different sectors. If an advisor expects yield spreads to narrow between agency, corporate, and mortgage-backed securities on the one hand, and Treasury securities on the other hand, the percentage of assets allocated to non-Treasury securities in the index fund is increased relative to the allocation contained in the benchmark. That is to say, Treasury securities are underweighted in the index fund. Conversely if the yield spreads are expected to widen, Treasury securities are overweighted.

The magnitude of incremental return that can be obtained through market sector selection depends on the volatility of sector spreads. Exhibit 5-1 is a graph of the historical nominal yield spreads between single-family current-coupon GNMA mortgage-backed securities and 10-year Treasury notes, and between 10-year single A industrial notes and 10-year Treasury notes.

As shown in the exhibit, the volatility of spreads can be significant. Between the first quarter of 1978 and the fourth quarter of 1981, the spread between mortgage-backed securities and Treasury securities quadrupled from about 70 basis points to about 280 basis points. In the corporate market, spread changes have been even more dramatic. Between the first quarter of 1978 and the second quarter of 1980, the spread between intermediate corporate and Treasury securities increased six-fold from about 30 basis points to

Exhibit 5-1. Historical Nominal Yield Spreads: Corporate and Mortgage-Backed Securities (1978-1989)

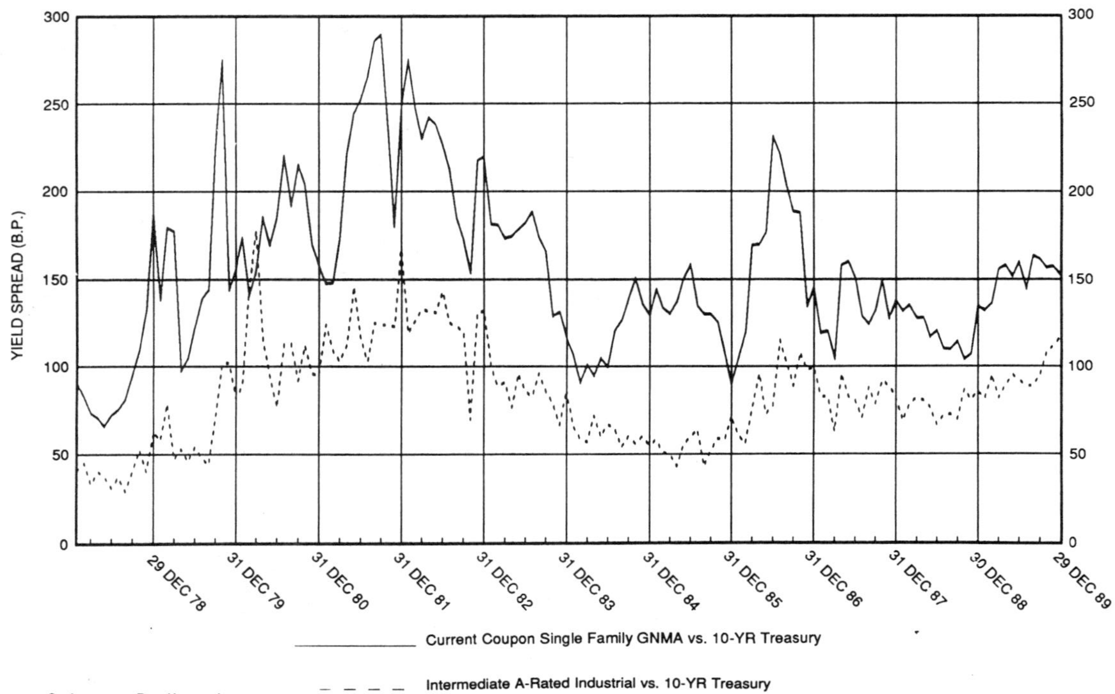

Source: Salomon Brothers Inc.

about 180 basis points. In both cases, overweighting of Treasury securities in the first quarter of 1978 would have increased the incremental return of a broad market index fund.

Incremental return—both expected as well as realized—can be measured by comparing the percentage share and effective duration of each underweighted and overweighted sector in the index fund to the percentage share and effective duration of each sector in the benchmark. For example, if an index fund advisor expects spreads in the 7- to 10-year maturity corporate sector to widen by 50 basis points relative to the 7- to 10-year maturity Treasury sector, the expected incremental return is determined by the relative overweighting and underweighting of each sector and by the effective duration of each sector. Exhibit 5-2 illustrates the impact of overweighting the Treasury sector and underweighting the corporate sector when spreads widen by 50 basis points.

In this exhibit, 7- to 10-year Treasury securities represent five percent, and 7- to 10-year corporate securities represent three percent of a broad market index. Since corporate spreads are expected to widen by 50 basis points, all securities in the 7- to 10-year corporate sector of the index fund are sold and replaced with similar Treasury securities. The swap out of corporate securities into Treasury securities is implemented while maintaining the combined share of the two 7- to 10-year sectors at eight percent and their combined contribution to the duration of the index fund at 0.44 years. Over a one-year horizon, the 7- to 10-year Treasury sector has an expected total return of 9.07 percent and the 7- to 10-year corporate sector has an expected total return of only 7.63 percent, a result of widening corporate spreads. The zero weighting of the 7- to 10-year corporate sector and the corresponding overweighting of the 7- to 10-year Treasury sector result in a contribution of 0.73 percent to the total return of the index fund, compared with a total return of 0.68 percent contributed by the 7- to 10-year Treasury and corporate securities in the benchmark. In this example, therefore, the expected incremental return is five basis points.

Similar overweighting and underweighting of all maturities in the Treasury, agency, corporate, and mortgage-backed securities sectors can result in significant outperformance (or underperform-

Exhibit 5-2: Incremental Return Due to Sector Selection and Changing Corporate Spreads

	Percent Held		Effective Duration		Expected Total Return[2]		Incremental Return
Sector	*Index*	*Index Fund*	*Index*	*Index Fund*	*Index*	*Index Fund*	
Treasury 7-10 years	5.0%	8.0%	5.8 yrs.	5.5 yrs.	9.07%	9.07%	—
Corporate 7-10 years	3.0	0.0	5.0	5.0	7.63	0.0	—
Contribution to Total[3]	8.0%	8.0%	0.44 yrs.	0.44 yrs.	0.68%	0.73%	+0.05

Notes:
1. Representative broad market index with 7-10 year corporates providing an extra yield of 1.01 percent.
2. Unchanged market environment except for corporate spreads widening by 50 basis points.
3. Contribution to total represents the contribution of the two Treasury and Corporate subsectors to the Index or Index fund totals.

ance) when yield spreads are volatile. Of course if yield spreads are expected to widen, longer-duration agency, corporate and mortgage-backed securities should be underweighted since they will experience a larger price loss relative to shorter-duration securities for the same widening of spreads.

While the strategy of deviating from the sector weights of a benchmark offers the potential for enhancing total returns, it is not risk-free. The risks of sector selection are twofold. First, if yield spreads do not change when the Treasury sector is overweighted, the index fund has foregone the incremental yield of agency, corporate, and mortgage-backed securities. For example, if 10 percent of the assets in the corporate sector are shifted to the Treasury sector when corporate securities have a higher average yield of say 100 basis points, the index fund will underperform its benchmark by about 10 basis points (100 basis points times 10 percent) for every year that yield spreads are unchanged.

Second, if yield spreads change in the opposite direction from what was expected, the index fund will underperform its benchmark. Thus, if corporate spreads tighten (rather than widen) by 50 basis points in Exhibit 5-2, the index fund will underperform its benchmark by an additional 10 basis points. As spreads tighten by 50 basis points, the corporate 7- to 10-year sector provides a total return of 12.63 percent. The contribution of the two 7- to 10-year sectors to the total return of the benchmark is 0.83 percent, compared with a total return of only 0.73 percent contributed by the two 7- to 10-year sectors in the index fund. The index fund has foregone the incremental yield as well as the price appreciation of the 7- to 10-year corporate sector. Of course, the risk of underperforming the benchmark in such an environment is greater if the corporate sector is underweighted significantly.

The risks of sector selection can be controlled by specifying the maximum amount of deviation from the sector weights of a particular index. A conservative enhanced index fund investor who is averse to the risk of underperforming a benchmark may allow very limited deviation. (It should be noted that reducing the maximum amount of deviation reduces the potential for incremental return.) The conservative enhanced index fund investor shown in Exhibit

5-3 allows the Treasury sector to be overweighted by a maximum of only five percent. If yield spreads widen in the corporate and mortgage-backed securities sector by 50 basis points (while the duration of each sector in the index fund matches the duration of each sector in the benchmark), the index fund could outperform, at best, by about three basis points.[1] If the aggressive enhanced index fund investor allows the Treasury sector to be overweighted by a maximum of 35 percent (to a maximum weight of 81 percent), the index fund could outperform by about 23 basis points.

The process of selecting market sectors applies to subsectors as well. In such an approach—referred to as "subsector selection"—the weight in the index fund of a subsector of the agency, corporate, and mortgage-backed securities sector deviates from the weight of the subsector in a benchmark. The overweighting or underweighting of each subsector need not impact the overall weight of the corresponding market sector. For example if the FFCB subsector is overweighted, the SLMA subsector can be underweighted and the agency sector, in aggregate, can have the same weight as the index.

Exhibit 5-3: Deviation in Sector Weights in Enhanced Index Funds

	*Percent Held in Index**	*Minimum-Maximum Deviation*		
		Conservative	*Neutral*	*Aggressive*
Treasury	46%	41-51%	37-55%	12-81%
Agency	8	7-9	6-10	0-24
Mortgage-Backed Securities	26	23-29	21-31	5-50
Corporate	20	18-22	16-24	4-40

*Representative broad market index.

1. Based on assumption that non-Treasury sectors provide, in aggregate, an extra yield of 145 basis points and that each sector had the characteristics of the broad market indexes as of December, 1989.

In fact, the agency sector can be overweighted or underweighted. Similarly, if industrial securities are underweighted, there is no requirement that the corporate sector be underweighted as well.

The opportunities for enhancing the returns of an index fund through subsector selection are significant since the yield spreads between subsectors, while not as volatile as yield spreads between broad market sectors, still fluctuate within a wide range. Exhibit 5-4 shows the yield spreads among subsectors in the agency market. The graph plots the yield spread between the 2-year FNMA subsector and the 2-year FFCB subsector between January of 1985 and December of 1986. Over a four-month period between June of 1985 and September of 1985, the yield spread between the two subsectors changed by more than 100 basis points. Prior to mid-1985, FNMA securities offered incremental yield, primarily due to investor concerns about the asset-liability mismatch at FNMA. However by mid-1985, investors had become more concerned about the health of the agricultural economy and the viability of the FFCB system. As a result, FFCB securities became less attractive to investors and the FFCB had to offer substantially higher yield levels than FNMA securities through late 1986.

The change in yield spreads between the two subsectors was much greater in short maturity securities. So while the yield spread between short FNMA and FFCB securities widened by more than 100 basis points, the yield spread between intermediate FNMA and FFCB securities widened by about 50 basis points. As spreads widened in FFCB securities, an index fund advisor could have overweighted FFCB securities relative to other agency securities. The returns of the index fund would have been enhanced by capturing both the incremental yield of FFCB securities as well as their price appreciation when FFCB securities yield levels were realigned with those of other agency securities.

Another large change in relative value among subsectors in the agency market occurred in 1988 when 30-year FICO securities offered an incremental yield of over 45 basis points relative to other agency securities. As shown in Exhibit 5-5, the incremental yield decreased rapidly between June of 1988 and February of 1989. Enhanced index funds could have captured the incremental yield as

Exhibit 5-4. Historical Yield Spreads: 2-Year Federal National Mortgage Association Security vs. 2-Year Federal Farm Credit Bank Security (1/1/85–12/31/86)

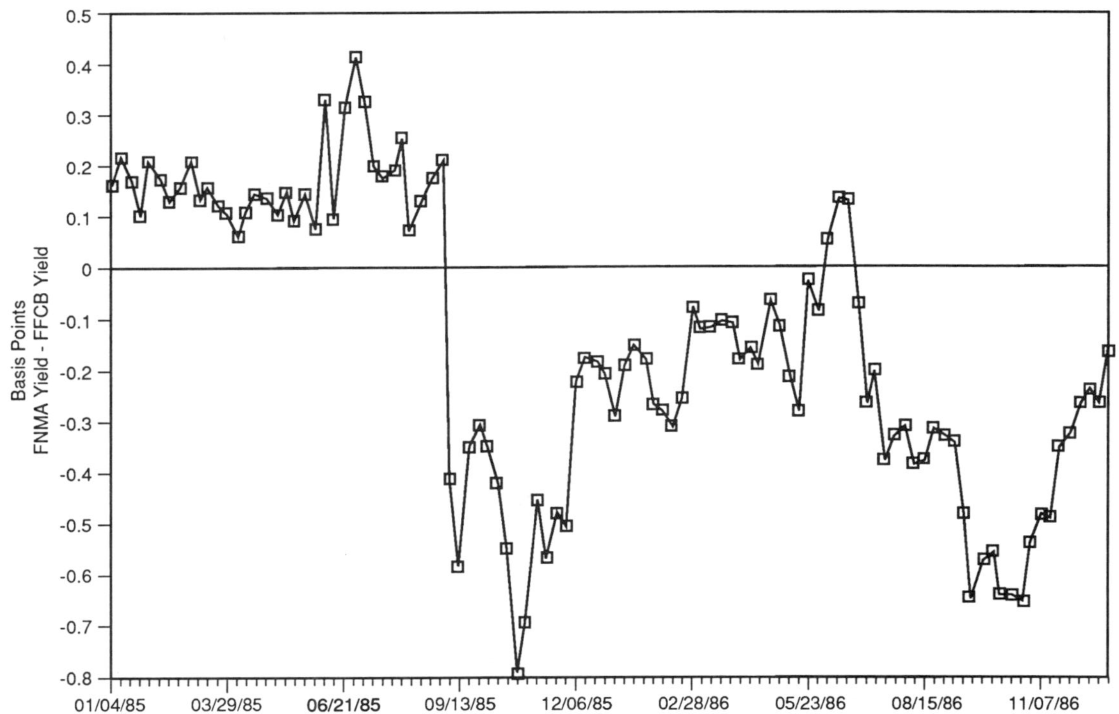

Source: Merrill Lynch Capital Markets.

Exhibit 5-5. Historical Yield Spreads: 30-Year Financing Corporation Security vs. 30-Year Federal National Mortgage Association Security (11/1/87–3/31/89)

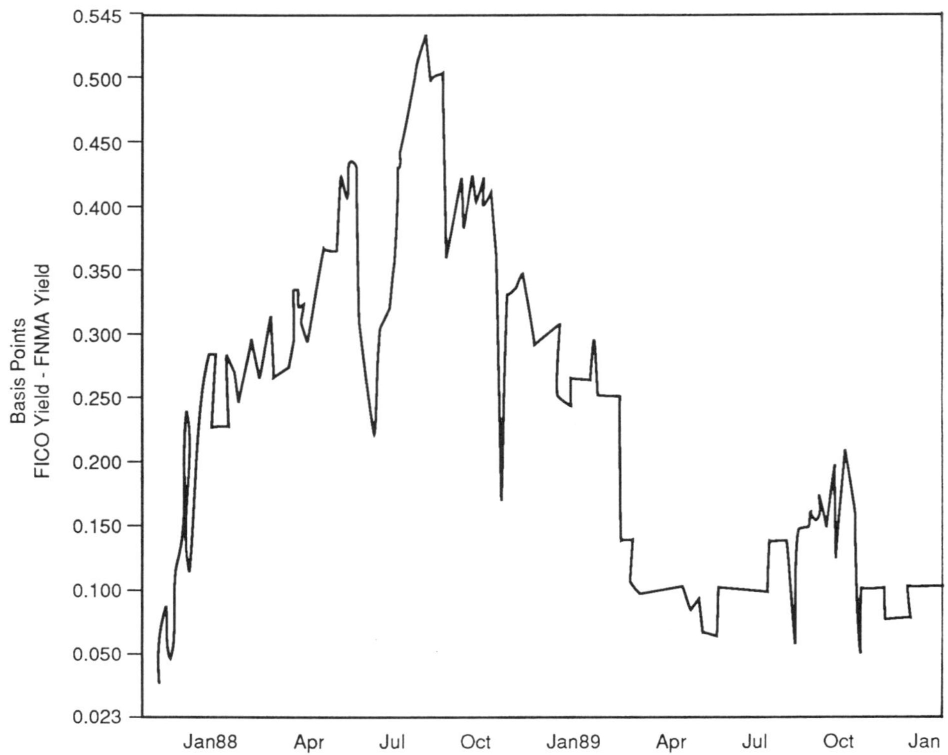

Source: Goldman Sachs & Co.

well as a price appreciation of about 4.5 percent relative to other 30-year agency securities.

In the corporate market, one of the greatest opportunities for subsector selection are found in changing credit quality spreads. As shown in Exhibit 5-6, the yield spread between higher credit quality corporate securities and lower credit quality corporate securities widens as the economy slows or enters a recession; conversely it narrows as the economy expands. The graph plots the ratio of the yield of AAA corporate securities to that of BAA corporate securities; the peak in this ratio (implying the smallest incremental yield from lower credit quality securities) often just lags the peak in the economic cycle. An index fund advisor can enhance the returns of an index fund by overweighting lower credit quality corporate subsectors in an expanding economy and overweighting higher credit quality corporate subsectors in a slowing economy.

Subsector selection among other subsectors in the corporate market—e.g., between utility securities and finance securities, or between industrial securities and Yankee securities—also provides opportunities for enhancing the returns of an index fund. Occasionally, the potential enhancement is significant. For example in the entire seven-year period ending in 1989, the yield spread between intermediate AA Yankee securities and intermediate AA industrial securities fluctuated within an 80-basis-point range. However, the majority of the time the yield spread between the two subsectors fluctuated within a 35-basis-point range only.

Subsector selection in the mortgage market offers similar opportunities for enhancing returns. Exhibit 5-7 illustrates the nominal yield spread between 30-year single-family current-coupon GNMA mortgage-backed securities and 30-year current-coupon FHLMC mortgage-backed securities. For the six-year period ending in 1989, the yield spread between the two subsectors fluctuated within a 68-basis-point range. Similar fluctuations can be observed in the yield spread between GNMA and FNMA mortgage-backed securities. The primary cause of such fluctuations has been changes in the supply of and the demand for certain types of mortgage-backed securities.

Finally, sector selection is not limited to market sectors and subsectors that are included in a benchmark. As discussed in Chap-

Exhibit 5-6. Historical Yield Ratio: AAA-Rated vs. BAA-Rated Seasoned Corporate Yields (1/1/69–12/31/89)

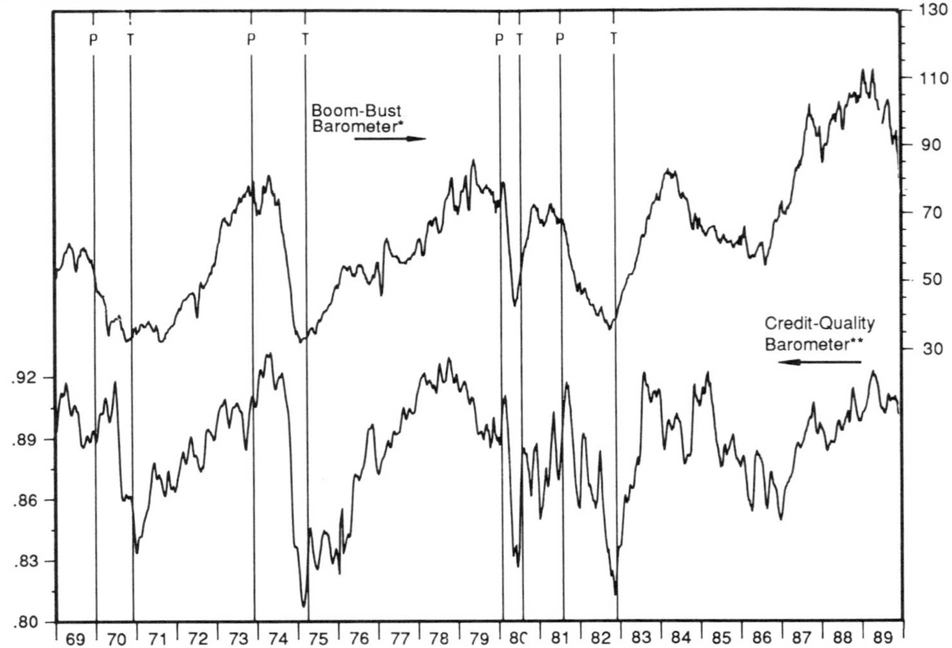

*CRB raw industrials spot prices divided by initial unemployment claims. All series shown are four-week moving averages.

** Moody's AAA/BAA seasoned corporate yields.

Source: Prudential Bache Securities.

Exhibit 5-7. Historical Nominal Yield Spreads: GNMA Current Coupon vs. FHLMC Current Coupon (7/15/83–12/31/89)

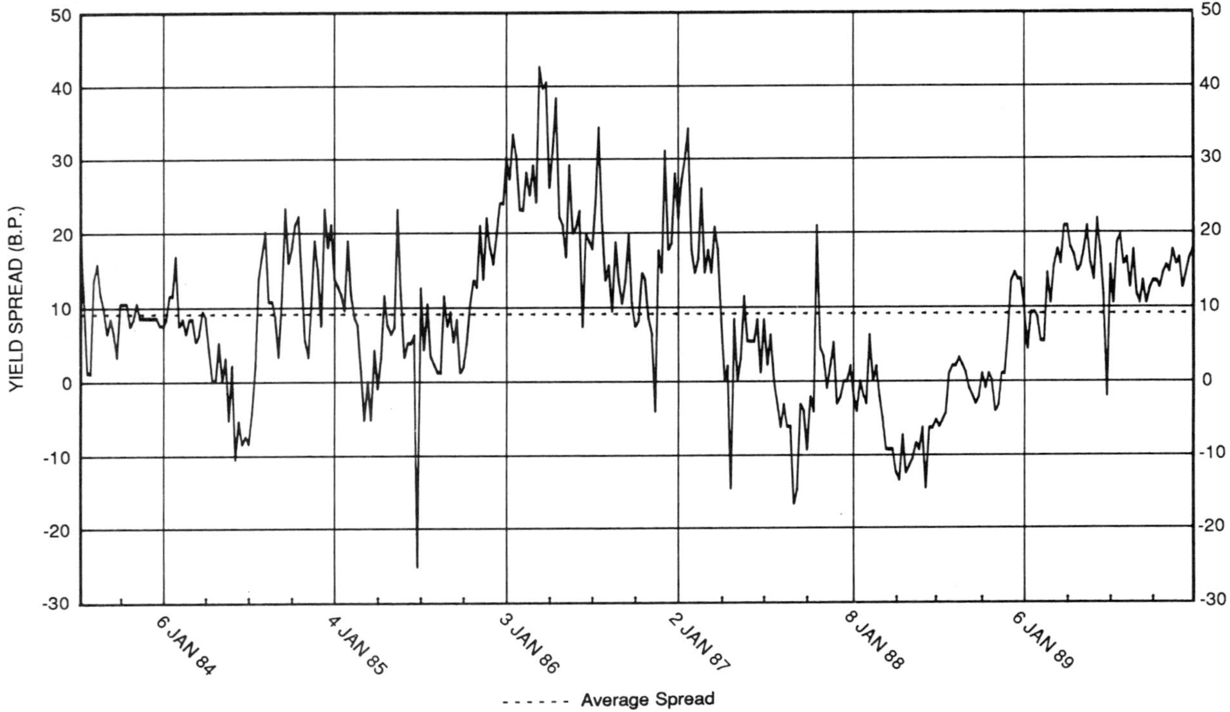

Source: Salomon Brothers Inc.

ter 1, there are several types of securities in the fixed income market that are not included in any of the broad market indexes. These sectors include zero coupon Treasury securities, medium-term notes, deposit notes, some asset-backed securities, private mortgage-backed securities and collateralized mortgage obligations (CMOs). An index fund advisor may choose to invest in these sectors to enhance the returns of an index fund; such sectors often have higher yield levels than their counterparts in market indexes. Furthermore, the downside in some sectors is limited because their yield spreads typically are highly correlated with the yield spreads of their counterparts in market indexes. Yield spreads of medium-term notes, for example, are correlated with the spreads of similar quality and similar type generic corporate securities.

An enhanced index fund advisor's decision to overweight or underweight different market sectors in enhanced index funds is comparable to an active investment advisor's decision to invest in or avoid different market sectors in traditional actively-managed portfolios. Both advisors examine the same factors to select market sectors with the highest expected returns—namely nominal and option-adjusted yield spreads, interest-rate volatility, supply and demand, and the economic environment.

For example, the decision to overweight or underweight mortgage-backed securities is affected by at least five factors: (i) the current level of yield spreads relative to historical levels; (ii) the expected level of volatility of interest rates; (iii) economic indicators such as housing construction, new home sales, housing turnover and mortgage rates, all of which impact the future supply and prepayment of mortgage-backed securities; (iv) the shape of the Treasury yield curve which affects the demand for mortgage-backed securities both directly and indirectly through its impact on the CMO market; and (v) any unique circumstance that may impact future supply and demand of mortgage-backed securities such as the changes in the risk-based capital guidelines for banks and thrifts, and the restructuring of the savings and loan industry begun in 1988.

Similar factors also are considered in the corporate sector. In addition to relative yield spreads and interest-rate volatility, an advisor considers the level of economic activity (since it affects the profitability of corporations) and any unique circumstance such as level of corporate restructuring or the secondary market for swapping the embedded options in callable corporate securities. It is important to emphasize that overweighting or underweighting a market sector is an active decision that requires sound judgement by an investment advisor, whether an enhanced index fund advisor or a traditional active investment advisor.

Maturity Sector Selection or Yield Curve Strategy

Maturity sector selection, also referred to as yield curve strategy, is another investment strategy with tremendous potential for enhancing the returns of an index fund. In maturity sector selection, an index fund advisor overweights or underweights different maturity sectors (in mortgage-backed securities, the maturity sector is based on the weighted average life of the mortgage pool rather than on the final maturity date) in an index fund relative to a benchmark to take advantage of shifts in the yield curve. Three alternative maturity sector selections are available: a "barbell" strategy in which short and long maturity sectors are overweighted while intermediate maturity sectors are underweighted; a "bullet" strategy in which, conversely, short- and long-maturity sectors are underweighted while intermediate-maturity sectors are overweighted; and a "neutral yield curve" strategy in which the maturity distribution of an index fund mirrors that of a benchmark. Like market sector selection, maturity sector selection is implemented while matching the duration of the enhanced index fund to that of a benchmark.

The decision to overweight or underweight a given maturity sector is based on an index fund advisor's expectation of future changes in the shape of the Treasury yield curve. If an advisor expects the Treasury yield curve to steepen (i.e., short-term rates fall more than long-term rates or short-term rates rise less than long-term rates), a bullet strategy is implemented. Conversely, if an advisor expects the Treasury yield curve to flatten or invert (i.e., short-term rates fall less than long-term rates or short-term rates rise more than long-term rates), a barbell strategy is implemented.

But, if the Treasury yield curve is expected to shift up or down parallel to its previous position (i.e., short-term rates change as much as long-term rates), any of the three yield curve strategies may be implemented. A barbell strategy is implemented if an advisor trades off the typically higher yield of a bullet maturity distribution for the greater convexity of a barbell maturity distribution. Often, a trade-off is made if the advisor expects large shifts in the yield curve in which the greater convexity, and consequently, the greater expected total return of the barbell maturity distribution offsets the foregone yield of the bullet maturity distribution. On the other hand, a bullet maturity distribution is implemented if such distribution either provides very high yield levels or offers average yield levels at a time when the advisor expects small shifts in the yield curve. Finally, a neutral yield curve strategy is implemented in the absence of compelling arguments for either a barbell or a bullet maturity distribution.

The total return of index funds can be enhanced significantly using yield curve strategies. Exhibit 5-8 illustrates the magnitude of changes in the shape of the Treasury yield curve: the graph plots the yield spread between 30-year Treasury bonds and 1-year Treasury bills.

One of the more notable opportunities for enhancing index fund total returns occurred between January of 1981 and December of 1982 when the slope of the Treasury yield curve shifted from an inverted negative 200 basis points to a steep positive 200 basis-point level. A bullet maturity distribution comprised of current coupon 10-year Treasury securities would have outperformed a duration-neutral barbell maturity distribution comprised of 3-month Treasury bills and current coupon 30-year Treasury securities by 5.3 percent over the two-year horizon (or 2.6 percent on an annualized basis).

A somewhat less significant opportunity occurred between January of 1988 and December of 1988. During this period as the slope of the yield curve changed from a steep level of 190 basis points to a flat level of zero basis points, a barbell maturity distribution of Treasury securities would have outperformed a duration-neutral bullet maturity distribution by 1.1 percent.

Exhibit 5-8. Historical Yield Spreads: 1-Year Maturity Treasury vs. 30-Year Maturity Treasury (1/31/79–12/31/89)

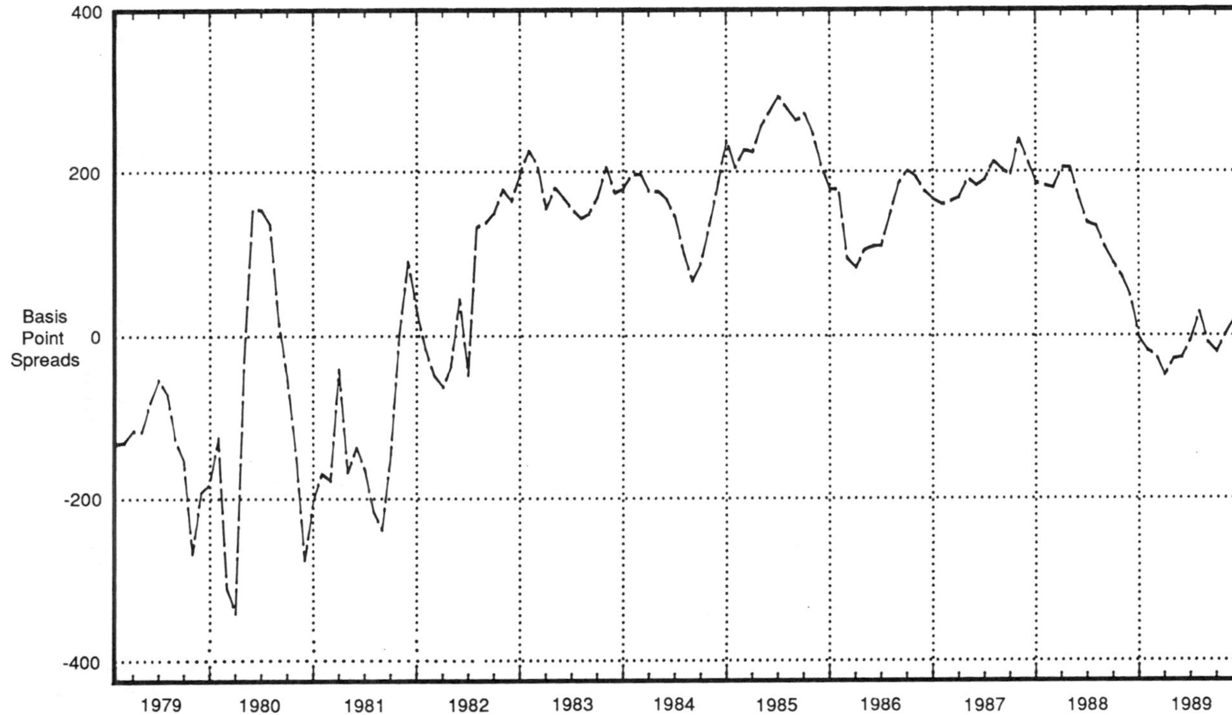

Source: Salomon Brothers Inc.

Like traditional active investment advisors, an index fund advisor's expectation of future changes in the shape of the Treasury yield curve is affected by several factors. They include: (i) the current shape of the Treasury yield curve relative to historical levels; (ii) interest rate volatility; (iii) current and expected Federal Reserve Bank policy; (iv) inflationary expectations; and (v) supply and demand considerations. Since an accurate prediction of the status of most of these factors is difficult, many index fund advisors limit the overweighting and underweighting of maturity sectors. For example, assets seldom are committed fully to a complete bullet or barbell maturity distribution. The risk of underperformance is high if an advisor has poor timing (too early or too late in implementing the strategy) or if an advisor implements the wrong strategy.

Coupon Selection

Coupon selection is the overweighting or underweighting of premium (high coupon), current coupon, or discount (low coupon) securities in an index fund relative to a benchmark. Two coupon selection strategies are available. The first applies to securities without embedded call and/or put options, and the second—and analytically more complex—applies to securities containing embedded call and/or put options.

The first coupon selection strategy is driven by the yield spreads between premium, current coupon, and discount securities. Coupon yield spreads can be very volatile as shown in Exhibit 5-9. The graph illustrates the spread between a premium Treasury security (13.75s of 5/15/92) and a discount Treasury security (7.25s of 8/15/92). In 1987 alone, the yield spread between the two issues widened to a high of 78 basis points and narrowed to a low of two basis points. In 1985, yield spreads fluctuated between 19 and 66 basis points. Given such volatility of yield spreads, the total return of an index fund can be enhanced by overweighting premium securities when yield spreads are wide and by underweighting premium securities when yield spreads are narrow.

Exhibit 5-9. Historical Yield Spreads: Premium versus Discount Treasury Securities 13.75% of 5/15/92 vs. 7.25% of 8/15/92

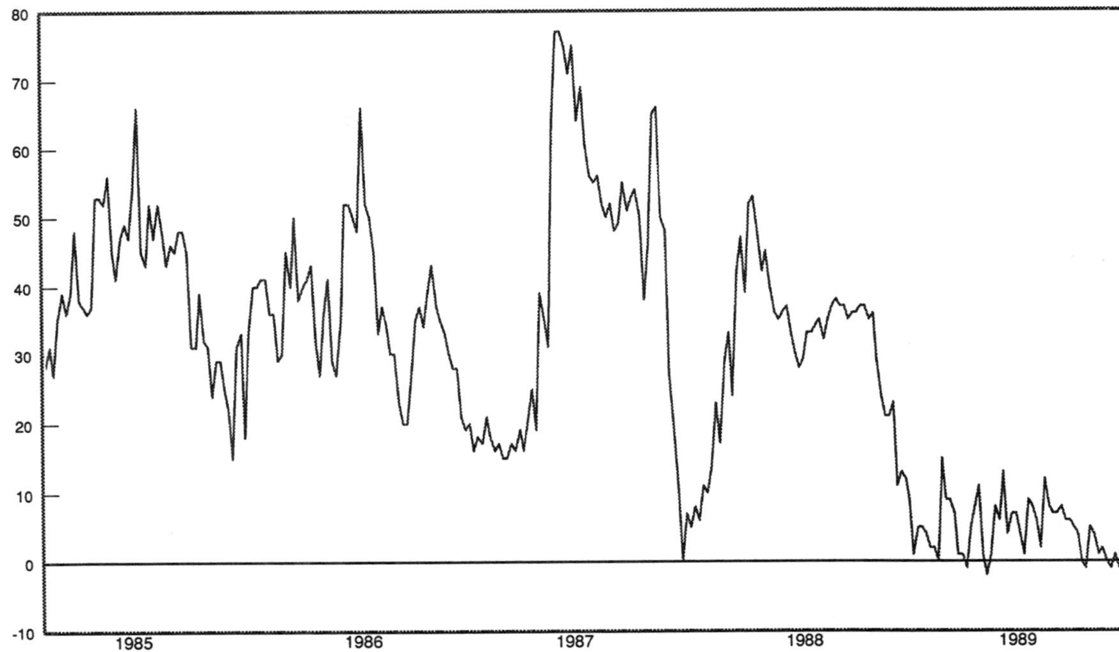

Source: Merrill Lynch Capital Markets.

The impact on total return of overweighting premium securities when yield spreads are relatively wide is twofold. The premium securities enhance returns by providing incremental yield, and also by appreciating in price relative to current coupon and discount securities as spreads narrow. For example, between June of 1985 and November of 1985, the premium 13.75s of 5/15/92 had a relative price appreciation of 2.2 percent, driven solely by narrowing spreads. Conversely, underweighting premium securities when yield spreads are relatively narrow enhances returns by avoiding the relative price depreciation of premium securities when yield spreads widen. So between February 1987 (when spreads between the 13.75s of 5/15/92 and the 7.25s of 8/15/92 stood at 15 basis points) and May of 1987 (when spreads stood at 76 basis points), the premium security had a price depreciation of 2.4 percent relative to the discount security.

Yield spreads between premium, current coupon, and discount securities are affected by different factors at different times. Sometimes the expected trend in the level of interest rates affects yield spreads. As interest rates decline, the realized compound yield (or effective yield) of premium securities also declines because large semi-annual coupon payments are reinvested at lower and lower rates.[2] The prospect of lower realized compound yield decreases the value of premium securities relative to current coupon and discount securities (the realized compound yield of current coupon and discount securities is not reduced as much by lower reinvestment rates), resulting in wider yield spreads between premiums, current coupons, and discounts. Similarly when interest rates rise, the realized compound yield of premium securities rises, increasing the value of premium securities relative to current coupon and discount securities. The increase in value implies narrower yield spreads.

The effect of the direction of interest-rate movements can be seen in the first half of 1985 when, as interest rates dropped, the spread between premium and discount securities more than doubled. (See Exhibit 5-9.) Similarly, as interest rates for short- and in-

2. Realized compound yield measures the impact of reinvestment rates on the future value of a security. For more information see Sidney Homer and Martin L. Leibowitz, *Inside the Yield Book*, Prentice-Hall, Inc., New Jersey, 1972.

termediate-maturity securities increased through most of 1988, the spread between premium and discount securities narrowed from 40 basis points to less than five basis points.

Realized compound yield, however, does not always account for changes in coupon yield spreads. In early 1987, interest rates rose and yet the spread between premium and current coupon and discount securities widened significantly. In this case, supply and demand imbalances accounted for the widening yield spreads.[3] During market rallies, investment advisors enter the market to capture price appreciation; they focus on liquid, readily available securities such as current coupon Treasury securities, triggering the widening of spreads between premium and current coupon securities.

Spreads often widen in the early phases of rising interest rate cycles as well. In the rally preceding a rising interest rate cycle, demand for current coupon securities outstrips available supply, prompting dealers to sell short current coupon Treasury securities. As interest rates rise, dealers cover their short sales thereby providing "technical support" for current coupon Treasury securities. Meanwhile, premium securities do not have the benefit of such technical support.

Finally, interest rate volatility also affects the coupon yield spread between premium, current coupon, and discount securities. When interest rate volatility is low, investment advisors focus on increasing the incremental yield of their portfolios. As investment advisors' demand for higher-yield premium securities increases, the spread decreases. The impact of lower interest rate volatility on coupon yield spreads can be seen in late 1985 and late 1986 (Exhibit 5-9).

While the returns of an index fund can be enhanced by taking advantage of volatile coupon yield spreads, the decision to overweight certain coupon levels is not a simple one. Direction of movement of interest rates, volatility of interest rates, and supply and

3. The impact of supply and demand imbalances has been examined by Edward L. Bishop and Mark Mahoney in "The Liquidity Premium of Current Issue Treasuries," Drexel Burnham Lambert Government Securities, Inc., February, 1988.

demand factors all have to be examined carefully before a prudent investment decision can be made.

The second coupon selection strategy is based on the option-adjusted yield spread between premium, current coupon, and discount securities with embedded call and/or put options. In this strategy, the index fund advisor overweights coupon levels with the highest option-adjusted spreads (often referred to as the OAS) at a given volatility level, irrespective of nominal yield spreads. Two factors account for different option-adjusted spreads among similar securities: different nominal yield spreads, and different (high or low) premiums for embedded call options or different (high or low) premiums for embedded put options.[4] If wider nominal spreads have led to high option-adjusted yield spreads for a particular coupon level, the securities will outperform securities with lower option-adjusted yield spreads as the nominal yield spreads narrow. On the other hand if high premiums account for the high option-adjusted yield spreads of callable securities, the securities will outperform as premiums for the embedded call options (that were, in effect, sold) decrease to appropriate market levels. If low premiums account for the high option-adjusted yield spreads of puttable securities, they will outperform as the premiums for the embedded put options increase to appropriate market levels.

This strategy may be implemented with corporate and mortgage-backed securities. In the corporate sector, high coupon callable securities have, at times, offered attractive nominal yield spreads but unattractive option-adjusted spreads relative to low coupon callable securities. Index fund advisors often will overweight high coupon securities and capture incremental yield if they expect low interest rate volatility or a rise in interest rates. If they expect high interest rate volatility or a decline in interest rates, index fund advisors will overweight low coupon securities and capture the better expected price performance of the securities with high option-adjusted spreads.

In the mortgage-backed securities sector, index fund advisors can make a similar trade-off between incremental nominal yield and

4. Premiums, in this context, refer to the price paid for options rather than to high coupon securities.

high option-adjusted spreads in selecting premium, current coupon or discount securities. A 1989 study by Salomon Brothers Inc. shows that returns of the mortgage component of index funds can be enhanced significantly—in some cases by as much as 155 basis points on an annualized basis—by selecting mortgage-backed securities with the highest option-adjusted spreads. Thus, if discount securities have the widest option-adjusted spreads, they should be overweighted relative to current coupon or premium securities. Alternatively, some investors track the historical price spread between different coupon level mortgage-backed securities as a guide to overweighting or underweighting premium, current coupon, or discount securities.

Irrespective of the approach used to select coupon levels in securities with embedded options, several factors have to be considered in coupon selection, including the expected trend in interest rates, volatility of interest rates, and changes in supply and demand. For example, in the early phases of a declining interest rate cycle, premium mortgage-backed securities tend to underperform discount mortgage-backed securities regardless of the option-adjusted spreads of the respective coupon levels. Enhanced index fund advisors concerned with the short-term realized tracking error of their portfolios, therefore, may decide not to overweight premium mortgage-backed securities because of the interim risk of wider nominal spreads. Similarly, anticipated demand for certain coupon levels for structuring CMOs often affects the short-term relative value of different coupon levels. Enhanced index fund advisors, therefore, may choose not to underweight certain coupon levels despite unfavorable option-adjusted spreads.

Issuer Selection

The corporate component of broad market indexes contains over 4,000 securities and 820 different issuers. Since an index fund cannot purchase a pro rata share of every corporate security, a diversified sample of corporate securities is selected to track the performance of the entire corporate component of broad market indexes. In enhanced index funds, however, issuer selection is used to select those corporate securities that are expected to outperform a diversified sample. Issuer selection—another investment strategy that can be used to enhance the total returns of an index fund—is the purchase and sale of corporate securities based on a corporation's current and expected credit standing. This strategy focuses on four types of investment-grade corporate issuers: low-credit quality issuers with stable ratings; low- and intermediate-credit quality issuers with improving ratings; all credit quality issuers with deteriorating ratings; and all credit quality issuers with notably different ratings published by Moody's Investors Services and Standard & Poor's Corporation.

Selecting securities from the first type of issuers—those with low but stable credit quality—enhances index fund total returns by providing incremental yield. Given a target credit quality distribution for each rating category, an enhanced index fund advisor can select securities with stable credit quality that are valued at the lower "notches" of the rating categories.

Selecting securities from the second type of issuers—those with low and intermediate but improving credit quality—enhances index fund total returns in two stages. Initially, these securities provide incremental yield. Eventually, price appreciation occurs relative to alternative securities as credit quality improves, the national rating agencies upgrade credit ratings, and credit spreads narrow. For example, an enhanced index fund advisor can select BBB securities that are trading at BBB yield spread levels but are expected to improve to A levels over time.

Securities from the third type of issuers—all issuers with deteriorating credit quality—should be avoided. Index fund total returns are enhanced by avoiding the widening of credit spreads and the consequent relative price depreciation. Thus, an enhanced index fund will benefit by selling (or avoiding) BBB securities that are trading at BBB yield spreads but are expected to fall below the critical investment-grade level.

Finally, index fund total returns can be enhanced by focusing on securities that are rated differently—by more than one notch—by Moody's Investor Services and by Standard & Poor's Corporation. If the securities are trading in line with the higher published quality rating while the enhanced index fund advisor concurs with the lower published quality rating, the securities should be sold and any potential price deterioration avoided. On the other hand, if the securities are trading in line with the lower published quality rating while the higher published quality rating is considered more realistic, the securities should be purchased in anticipation of the expected market reevaluation and relative price appreciation.

It should be noted that while issuer selection can enhance the total returns of an index fund, the subsector selection within the corporate market—selection of industrial, utility, bank and finance, and Yankee subsectors, as well as selection of AAA, AA, A and BBB subsectors—typically has a greater impact than issuer selection on total return. Corporate subsector selection, therefore, takes precedence over issuer selection. If the long-maturity component of the BBB sector is eliminated from the index fund because of widening quality spreads and an impending recession, issuer selection in the long-maturity BBB rating category becomes moot.

Arbitrage

The total returns of index funds can be enhanced through arbitrage. Arbitrage is the simultaneous purchase and sale of equivalent securities to take advantage of price discrepancies between those securities. Arbitrage opportunities occur in all sectors of the cash market as well as in the derivatives market.

Price discrepancies in the cash market are due primarily to technical conditions, notably long and short positions in specific securities among dealers, demand for collateral for stripping purposes or for creating CMO's, and demand for particular securities by dealers working as agents on behalf of other investment advisors.

Short and long positions often provide the greatest arbitrage opportunities. Short dealer positions translate into aggressive bids for corporate securities when a dealer covering a short position quotes a bid price substantially higher than the price of other dealers and of comparable securities. Short and long positions also prompt dealers to offer attractive swaps between comparable corporate securities where an investment advisor can capture as much as 20 basis points of incremental yield. In the Treasury and agency sectors, the magnitude of price discrepancies or of incremental yield is much less. If a dealer has shorted a particular Treasury STRIPS, the dealer may propose a swap out of that security into a "neighboring" STRIPS (maturity difference of no more than three months) for less than five basis points of incremental yield relative to the rest of the market.

In the mortgage-backed securities sector, frequent arbitrage opportunities exist in the forward roll market in which an advisor sells securities for settlement in the current month and purchases the same securities for settlement in the forward month at a lower price. At times the forward price is significantly lower, offsetting the foregone yield of mortgage-backed securities relative to the yield of short-term investments, providing an incremental return of several hundred basis points on an annualized basis. Opportunities in the forward roll market are a function of several factors, including activity in the CMO market, the volume of mortgage issuance by bankers who seek to hedge their issuance in the forward market, and the shape of the Treasury yield curve.

Arbitrage opportunities in the derivatives market are due primarily to supply and demand conditions as well. In the futures market, the price discrepancy (known as the basis) between the bond futures contract and the underlying cheapest-to-deliver Treasury security can fluctuate, and the futures contract may be rich or cheap. The magnitude of incremental return from arbitrage in the futures market varied significantly in the 1980's. The incremental return was greatest in 1985 when bond futures outperformed a similar duration portfolio of all Treasury securities with a maturity of 20 or more years by over five percent; in 1986, bond futures underperformed by about two percent. More recently, the magnitude of the arbitrage has diminished. In 1988, bond futures outperformed the cheapest-to-deliver Treasury securities by about 80 basis points.

The diminished opportunities in the above arbitrage can be seen in Exhibit 5-10. As shown in this exhibit, the price discrepancy

Exhibit 5-10. Arbitrage Between Bond Futures Contract and Cheapest-to-Deliver Treasury

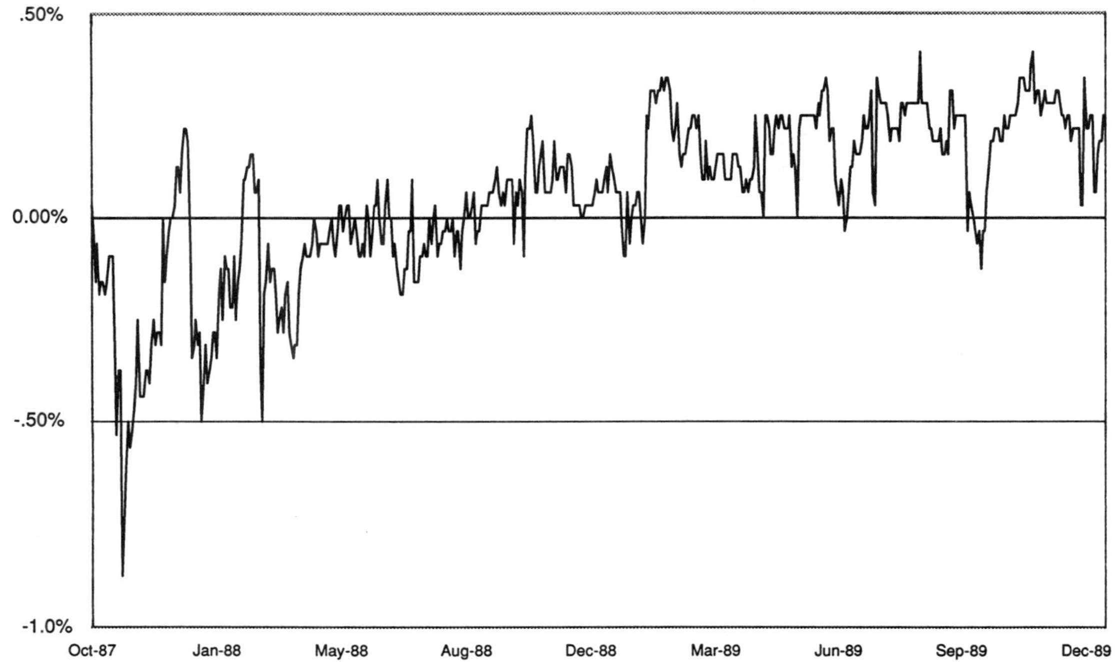

Source: Kidder, Peabody & Co. Inc.

between the bond futures contract and the cheapest-to-deliver Treasury security—after adjusting for the value of the embedded delivery and "wild card" options—ranged between negative 6 basis points and positive 41 basis points in the 12-month period ending 1989.

The key requirements for taking advantage of arbitrage opportunities to enhance index fund total returns are a high degree of active daily involvement in the fixed income market, good judgement and fast action on the part of the index fund advisor. Many of the opportunities are fleeting ones; an aggressive bid by a dealer with a short position is withdrawn as soon as the short position has been covered. An aggressive offering is snapped up quickly. In the derivatives market, richness and cheapness in the bond and note futures contracts disappear quickly as well because arbitrageurs typically force the contracts to fair value in a short period of time.

Enhanced Indexing Versus Risk-Control and Sector Rotation

Risk- (or duration-) control and sector rotation are two fixed income investment disciplines that have been developed in response to the relative underperformance of traditional fixed income disciplines based on forecasting interest rates. In risk-control, a portfolio is constrained to match certain risk parameters of a selected benchmark; the parameters include, at minimum, a duration level and, often, some quality and sector distribution as well. The objective of the investment discipline is to outperform a selected benchmark while matching some of the risk characteristics of that benchmark. In sector rotation, a portfolio is constrained such that only the portfolio's duration matches that of a selected benchmark. The objective of the investment discipline is to outperform a selected benchmark while matching the duration of that benchmark.

Thus, the difference between risk-control and sector rotation is twofold. First, in sector rotation the portfolio is constrained by duration and not by quality and sector distributions. Second, in sector rotation the objective is to outperform a benchmark primarily by taking advantage of sector selection only and not by using multiple investment strategies.

Common bonds tie risk-control and sector rotation to enhanced indexing. In all three disciplines, the duration of the portfolio tracks the duration of a selected benchmark. In all three, sector selection and maturity selection are significant in providing incremental return. In two disciplines—risk-control and enhanced indexing—quality and sector constraints are implemented. Given the same benchmark, a risk-control portfolio with many conservative risk parameter constraints and an enhanced index fund with very aggressive risk parameter constraints may be indistinguishable. Furthermore, in risk-control and in enhanced indexing, the same investment strategies may be used to outperform a selected benchmark. The three investment disciplines thus may be viewed as situated along a spectrum of increasing risk with enhanced indexing as the discipline constrained by the greatest number of risk parameters and with the lowest risk relative to a benchmark. Risk-control comes next, followed by sector rotation.

There are two additional differences between enhanced indexing, and risk-control and sector rotation: expected incremental return and fees. In enhanced indexing, the expected annual incremental return above the benchmark is no more than 50 basis points. In risk-control and sector rotation, over 100 basis points is expected. And in enhanced indexing, the fees are about half those of risk-control and sector rotation. The fees on the latter investment disciplines are more in line with those of traditional active managers.

Choosing Between Enhanced and Pure Indexing

Given the potential for enhancing the total return of index funds by 25—and sometimes as much as 50—basis points, the question arises as to why an index fund investor would choose pure index funds. Two factors account for the choice. First, while enhanced index funds are expected to outperform their benchmarks over a market cycle, they may underperform during interim periods. The investment strategies described earlier in the chapter may require extended periods to succeed, and sometimes they do not succeed at all. Many index fund investors are not willing to accept the risk of interim underperformance.

Second, the fees for enhanced indexing are higher than those for pure indexing. Fees alone, however, should not deter index fund investors from selecting enhanced indexing. The additional cost is usually less than 10 basis points. And even in cases where 10 basis points seems too high, incentive (performance-based) fees can be used so that the full additional cost is paid only when the index fund has outperformed the benchmark by a certain predetermined amount.

Chapter 6

Implications of Indexing for the Fixed Income Market

Increased use of bond indexing will have a far-reaching impact on the fixed income market. Already, profit margins throughout the investment community are showing signs of being squeezed. Investment advisors increasingly will be forced to accept lower management fees, financial consultants will be retained less frequently to conduct searches for new investment advisors, and the broker/dealer community will face the tightening of bid-ask price spreads. At the same time, short-term market volatility and trading volume will decline with lower portfolio turnover and the absence of "market timing" trades in index funds. Ultimately, increased indexing will lead to a significant shakeout among investment advisors. The beneficiaries of such a shakeout will be firms with large assets as well as established specialty boutiques; the casualties will be smaller organizations without extensive resources or particular niches.

Declining Profit Margins

Proliferation of indexing will squeeze profit margins throughout the investment community. The losers will be investment advisors, consultants, and broker/dealers. The winners will be pension plan sponsors, endowment sponsors, and other investors who invest in index funds.

Investment advisors will be squeezed by a combination of lower advisory fees and higher expenses associated with managing pure index and enhanced index funds. As discussed in Chapter 1, advisory fees for index funds are low and range between 30 and 75 percent of advisory fees for actively-managed portfolios. Moreover, as the competition among index fund advisors intensifies, investment advisors will attempt to differentiate themselves—and to retain an edge—through even lower advisory fees.

Compounding the impact of lower fees are the higher expenses associated with the management of index funds. These expenses can be substantial. Extensive portfolio analysis systems are required to manage an index fund in order to control the risk and return parameters of an index fund relative to a selected benchmark. Acquiring and maintaining such systems require costly staff, expensive computer hardware and software, pricing data, communication systems, and, in some instances, vendor computer processing costs.

Additionally, successful index fund advisors must have comprehensive performance attribution capabilities to explain and document the source of the realized tracking error of pure index funds and of the value added of enhanced index funds. Developing and maintaining such capabilities—which are not required to the same extent in actively-managed portfolios—represent additional expenses.

The profit squeeze stemming from lower fees and higher expenses is greatest for small-sized index funds. Economies of scale begin to set in for index funds larger than, say, $100 million; that is to say, after critical size is reached, expenses no longer increase in the same proportion as the size of the index fund. The benefits of larger index funds both to investors and to index fund advisors thus will encourage the use of commingled—or pooled—index funds.

Wider use of indexing will reduce the amount of business available to consultants as well. With lower turnover of investment advisors, consultants will be retained less frequently to conduct searches for new investment advisors. Indeed, having opted for fixed income indexing, investors may conduct a search for an index fund advisor directly and without the benefit of a consultant. Some investors perceive indexing—particularly pure indexing—as a commodity-like service that can be purchased from any of many key large index fund advisors. These investors will select an index fund advisor directly based on the level of fees and on their own assessment of the capabilities of the index fund advisors—evaluating both the structure of the investment organization and the individual advisors.

Broker/dealer profit margins will decline as indexing leads to tighter bid-ask spreads, particularly in the government and non-derivative mortgage-backed securities sectors. Two factors account for the tighter bid-ask spreads. First, index fund advisors are extremely sensitive to transaction costs, since such costs diminish the total return of an index fund. The magnitude of the decrease depends on the level of portfolio turnover and on the type of securities traded. For example, as discussed in Chapter 4, transaction costs can reduce the total return of a broad index fund by as much as 40 basis points annually with an average monthly turnover of 11 percent.

The transaction costs used in calculating the total return of market indexes do not reflect accurately the transaction costs incurred by bond index funds. The only transaction costs estimated and incorporated in market indexes are those associated with adding newly-issued securities to the index universe. Between 1980 and 1989, the dollar amount outstanding of securities in broad market indexes grew by 29 percent a year on average from new issuance.[1] Most of this growth had been in the government and mortgage-backed securities sectors, both of which have lower transaction costs than the corporate sector. Assuming transaction costs of between one-sixteenth and one-quarter of a point for new-issue government, mortgage-backed, and corporate securities, a 29 percent growth rate results in a transaction-cost drag on total return of between three and five basis points a year. Such costs are dwarfed by the costs

1. The growth from new issuance was partially offset by the removal of securities due to maturation, redemption, or downgrading of credit rating to below investment-grade. The net growth of the dollar amount outstanding of securities in broad market indexes was about 15 percent a year between 1980 and 1989.

incurred in actual index funds. First, broad market index funds have higher portfolio turnover rates than 29 percent a year; second, the turnover in index funds is not overweighted by current coupon government and mortgage-backed securities; and third, unlike broad market indexes, index fund advisors have to reinvest income and principal payments generated by the portfolio by purchasing securities at the ask price.

Thus, index fund advisors have become extremely sensitive to the bid-ask spreads of their transactions as they attempt to minimize the drag on total return. Typically, index fund advisors shop around among several dealers, seeking the lowest ask and highest bid price for their transactions and effectively narrowing the bid-ask spreads at which trades are executed. It should be noted, however, that the bid-ask spread from any one dealer may remain wider than the spread between the lowest ask and highest bid price available in the market.

The extreme bid-ask spread sensitivity of enhanced index fund advisors also is partly explained by the amount of value added by indexing. An enhanced index fund is expected to return between 25 and 75 basis points a year above its benchmark depending on the size of assets, type of index fund, and style of index fund advisor. The incremental return expected from a conservatively-managed, low-turnover (under 50 percent a year) broad market index fund may total 25 basis points. Bid-ask spreads can reduce the incremental return by six to 12 basis points; at the higher level, transaction costs thus can total one-half of the incremental return of the index fund. Similarly, the incremental return of an aggressively-managed, high-turnover (over 100 percent a year) broad market index fund may total 75 basis points. Transaction costs of as much as 40 basis points (see Chapter 4) represent over one-half the incremental return of the index fund. Transaction costs, therefore, are sizeable relative to the incremental return of index funds. In traditional actively-managed portfolios, on the other hand, transaction costs are much smaller relative to the expected incremental return. So the greater the proportion of transaction costs, the greater the sensitivity to bid-ask spreads.

A second factor contributing to tighter bid-ask spreads is the index fund advisor's reduced dependence on the broker/dealer community for such services as economic analysis, extensive research, and market sector and security valuation. Index fund advisors, particularly pure index fund advisors, do not rely on Wall Street economists and their data to the same extent as traditional active managers. In addition, most index fund advisors have extensive security and portfolio analysis systems to evaluate the complex cash flows of individual securities, and to control the risk and return parameters of their portfolios. Since most of these systems are not obtained from the broker/dealer community, the reliance of the index fund advisors on Wall Street research and services is reduced. Index fund advisors, therefore, are less inclined to accept wide bid-ask spreads as payment for research and services that are of lower value to them.

Broker/dealer profits will decline not only because of tighter bid-ask spreads, but also because of lower portfolio turnover. Index funds typically experience lower turnover rates than traditional actively-managed portfolios, and among index funds, pure index funds have lower turnover rates than do enhanced index funds. For example, as shown in Exhibit 6-1, a typical government bond portfolio actively managed by investment advisors or mutual fund managers has had average annual turnover rates of over 150 percent and as high as 380 percent in recent years. Turnover rates for pure and enhanced government index funds rarely will exceed 30 and 50 percent respectively. Turnover rates are about 40 percent for a typical $100 million pure broad market index fund and about 70 percent for a similar-sized enhanced index fund. Lower turnover rates, in turn, imply fewer opportunities for broker/dealers to capture the already tight bid-ask spreads, leading to a further squeeze on profits.

Decline in Market Volatility and Liquidity

Increased indexing will decrease short-term volatility in the fixed income market. The risk and return parameters of pure index funds closely track those of the benchmark, significantly reducing the pure

Exhibit 6-1. Average Annual Portfolio Turnover

Type of Institution	*Government Bond Portfolio*		*Corporate Bond Portfolio*		*Mortgage-Backed Securities Portfolio*	
	1988	*1989*	*1988*	*1989*	*1988*	*1989*
Investment Advisors	184	154	118	95	122	116
Mutual Fund Managers	381	225	51	48	Not available	

Source: Greenwich Associates, "Warning: Tricky Undercurrents," 1989.

index fund advisor's concerns about changes in interest rates, shifts in the shape of the Treasury yield curve, widening and narrowing of sector spreads, and fluctuations in interest-rate volatility. Pure index fund advisors, therefore, are not reactive to day-to-day market changes. Enhanced index fund advisors too, while somewhat more reactive to day-to-day changes in the fixed income market, still are less reactive than traditional active managers. Enhanced index fund advisors often maintain a neutral position relative to a benchmark, not overweighting or underweighting any sector, maturity distribution, quality or coupon. For example, the release of economic indicators—which results in some of the most volatile trading sessions in the fixed income market—will not prompt most pure and enhanced index fund advisors to lengthen or shorten their portfolio durations. Indexing, therefore, will reduce the intensity with which the market rises or falls on such occasions; this contrasts sharply with the tendency of portfolio insurance to magnify initially small price swings into large ones.

Decreased volatility combined with lower portfolio turnover will affect liquidity in certain sectors of the market. Broker/dealers benefit from trading opportunities stemming from market volatility and portfolio turnover. In the absence of volatility and portfolio turnover, broker/dealers will be reluctant to bid on securities they may have to hold for a long time; similarly, these broker/dealers will be reluctant to sell short securities they may not be able to purchase readily at a later date. Such reluctance to trade will translate into greater illiquidity in such market sectors as corporates, specific mortgage-backed securities, and derivative securities.

Impending Shakeout Among Investment Advisors

The shakeout within the investment advisory community will be triggered by the need for fewer investment advisors when indexing assets. The size of assets given to any single advisor for index fund management generally is much larger than the size of assets given to any single advisor for active management. Indexing, therefore, typically results in a consolidation of advisors responsible for managing a given pool of assets.

Following such consolidation, the entire investment advisory community will experience much lower turnover. Investors are less likely to terminate their index fund advisors since the risk is low of egregious underperformance. Lower termination rates and lower turnover imply fewer—but more intense—opportunities for investment advisors to woo each other's clients.

The beneficiary of consolidation will be the investment advisory organization with large assets. The fixed income market matured significantly, and market sectors and securities became more efficiently priced in the 1980's due to the proliferation of quantitative analysis, arbitrage theories, and sophisticated investment advisors. Thus, adding value to an index fund has become more and more difficult. Providing incremental total return above a benchmark not only requires investment expertise and experience but also substantial resources including quantitative analysts, credit research analysts, market sector specialists, traders, security and portfolio analysis systems, and performance attribution systems. Moreover, to be successful, index fund advisors must have the capability of designing and maintaining customized benchmarks. Only large organizations with sizeable assets under management can provide all the resources needed to support a successful index fund operation.

Small asset size restricts the ability to execute trades efficiently. Small asset size, for example, often results in odd-lot and, therefore, costly transactions that create a drag on the performance of index funds. Small assets size also limits the investment opportunities available to an index fund advisor. Most broker/dealers give priority to preferred (read large) investment advisor clients in offering or bidding for securities at attractive prices.

Secondary Effects

Increased indexing will have secondary effects on the fixed income market. The proliferation of indexing will hinder some organizations—especially smaller ones—from successfully introducing innovative, non-indexing fixed income strategies. The value added by any new strategy will have to be large enough to offset the consistent performance, the relatively low risk and the low fees of indexing. In the absence of an actual track record, simulated historical performance data has to be comprehensive, unbiased, and unquestionably realistic to overcome the skepticism shown toward back-tested strategies. And a new product has to be marketed broadly over a long period of time. The lead time required by investors to shift assets away from an index fund into a new fixed income strategy will, therefore, increase. Investment advisory organizations with the staff to design such strategies, the resources to provide credible simulated data and the staying power to withstand the long lead times will be few.

Another secondary effect will be the increased use and refinement of portfolio and benchmark analysis systems. Measuring the risk and return parameters of portfolios and benchmarks is the most critical step in index fund management. The need for systems that can measure such parameters accurately, frequently, and in an efficient manner is great. Portfolio analysis systems may be developed by index fund advisors internally, by broker/dealers who benefit from the trades resulting from the restructuring and rebalancing of index funds, or by third-party software vendors.

Performance attribution systems will improve also. Enhanced index fund advisors will be required to account for the incremental return of their index funds, attributing performance on a monthly or quarterly basis to any number of strategies. If an index fund has outperformed its benchmark by, say, 15 basis points in any one month, the advisor will be called to account for the source of each basis point of performance differential. The advisor must measure the net impact of deviations in market sector weightings, in maturity distribution, and in credit quality as well as the net effect of issue selection, of pricing errors, and of transaction costs. Given the number of possible variables and difficulties in quantifying some key variables, the task becomes a complex and tedious one for which reliable systems have not yet been developed.

To conclude, indexing has established itself as an attractive, low-cost approach to fixed income investments since the mid-1980's. Increasingly, corporate and public retirement funds, endowments, and even individual investors (through mutual funds) are turning to indexing. As the size of assets invested in index funds continues to grow, the fixed income market will experience significant changes. Some of these changes have begun to take hold, namely lower portfolio turnover, tighter bid-ask spreads, lower advisory fees and greater emphasis on performance attribution. The shake-out of the investment advisory community, on the other hand, will take longer to play itself out. Still, there is no doubt that it will come. The investment community should focus on the implications of indexing and better prepare itself for success in an increasingly competitive market.

Appendix A

Major U.S. Investors in Bond Index Funds

The table which follows lists U.S. index fund investors with over $250 million each committed to pure and enhanced bond index funds as of January 1, 1990. The assets represent corporate, public, and multiple employer pension plans, retiree medical benefit plans and endowments. Assets committed to index funds in the form of asset allocation or balanced funds are not included since these assets can be taken out of bond index funds and invested into equity securities or held in cash or cash equivalent securities. Bond index commingled pools and mutual funds which included multiple investors are not included. The assets covered in the table total $61 billion, represent twenty-seven investors, and thirty-two investment management organizations.

Major U.S. Investors in Bond Index Funds

Index Fund Investor[a]	*Size of Indexed Assets (millions as of 1/1/90)*	*Index(es)*[a]	*Investment Advisor(s)*[a]
New York City Retirement Systems	$22,271	Components of Salomon Brothers Targeted Index Matrix Core ⊕ 5	Bankers Trust Company BEA Associates, Inc. Bear Stearns Asset Management Chase Investors Management Corporation Fiduciary Trust Company International Fischer, Francis, Trees & Watts, Inc. Investment Advisers, Inc. Kennedy Associates, Inc. Lehman Ark Management Co., Inc. Lincoln Capital Management Company Mellon Bond Associates Miller, Anderson & Sherrerd Mitchell Hutchins Asset Management Inc. Pacific Investment Management Company The Putnam Companies, Inc. RCM Capital Management State Street Bank & Trust Company T. Rowe Price Associates, Inc. Weiss, Peck & Greer Wells Fargo Investment Advisors WR Lazard & Co.

Index Fund Investor[a]	*Size of Indexed Assets (millions as of 1/1/90)*	*Index(es)*[a]	*Investment Advisor(s)*[a]
California State Teachers' Retirement System	$13,256	Salomon Brothers Large Pension Fund Baseline Bond Index	In-House
AT&T Master Pension Trust	$ 4,131	Salomon Brothers Broad Investment-Grade Bond Index	Jennison Associates Capital Corp.
Virginia Supplemental Retirement System	$3,150	Lehman Brothers Government/Corporate Bond Index Lehman Brothers Long Government/Corporate Bond Index Merrill Lynch Corporate and Government Master (1-3 years)	MacKay-Shields Financial Corporation Massachusetts Financial Services Merganser Capital Management Corp. Sanford C. Bernstein & Co., Inc. Security Capital Management Inc. Sovran Capital Management Corporation Western Asset Management Company
Florida State Board of Administration	$2,250	Lehman Brothers Customized Index	In-House
Pennsylvania Public School Employees Retirement System	$ 2,090	Lehman Brothers Aggregate Bond Index Lehman Brothers Intermediate Government/Corporate Bond Index	In-House Mellon Bond Associates
NYNEX Corporation Master Pension Trust	$ 1,353	Salomon Brothers Broad Investment-Grade Bond Index Lehman Brothers Treasury Index	In-House Jennison Associates Capital Corp.

(table continues)

Index Fund Investor[a]	*Size of Indexed Assets (millions as of 1/1/90)*	*Index(es)*[a]	*Investment Advisor(s)*[a]
Public Employees' Retirement System of Mississippi	$ 1,308	Lehman Brothers Aggregate Bond Index Lehman Brothers Government/ Corporate Bond Index	Mellon Bond Associates Wells Fargo Investment Advisors
Minnesota State Board of Investment	$ 998	Salomon Brothers Broad Investment-Grade Bond Index	Fidelity Management Trust Company Lincoln Capital Management Company
Illinois Teachers' Retirement System	$ 889	Salomon Brothers Broad Investment-Grade Bond Index Lehman Brothers Intermediate Government/Corporate Bond Index	State Street Bank & Trust Company
Indiana Public Employees' Retirement System	$ 855	Salomon Brothers Broad Investment-Grade Bond Index	Prime Capital Management, Inc.
Arizona State Retirement System	$ 671	Lehman Brothers Aggregate Bond Index	Wells Fargo Investment Advisors
Washington State Investment Board	$ 664	Lehman Brothers Government/ Corporate Bond Index	In-House
Pennsylvania State Employees' Retirement System	$ 599	Lehman Brothers Aggregate Bond Index	Mellon Bond Associates

Index Fund Investor[a]	*Size of Indexed Assets (millions as of 1/1/90)*	*Index(es)*[a]	*Investment Advisor(s)*[a]
AMERITECH Pension Trust	$ 588	Salomon Brothers Broad Investment-Grade Bond Index Lehman Brothers Government/Corporate Bond Index	First Wisconsin Trust Company Lincoln Capital Management Company
Westinghouse Electric Corporation Master Trust	$ 530	Lehman Brothers Government/Corporate Bond Index	Westinghouse Pension Investment Corporation
Exxon U.S. Annuity Plans	$ 520	Salomon Brothers Targeted Index Matrix Core ⊕ 5	In-House Chase Investors Management Corporation
United Mine Workers of America Health and Retirement Funds	$ 520	Lehman Brothers Government/Corporate Bond Index	In-House
Maryland State Retirement & Pension Systems	$ 366	Salomon Brothers Broad Investment-Grade Bond Index	In-House
Illinois State Universities' Retirement System	$ 305	Salomon Brothers Broad Investment-Grade Bond Index	Wells Fargo Investment Advisors
Massachusetts Pension Reserves Investment Management Board	$ 287	Lehman Brothers Government Corporate Bond Index	Lehman Ark Management Co. Inc.
CBS Inc.	$ 257	Lehman Brothers Government/Corporate Bond Index Ten-Year Treasury Index	Fidelity Management Trust Company Lehman Ark Management, Co., Inc.

(table continued)

Index Fund Investor[a]	*Size of Indexed Assets (millions as of 1/1/90)*	*Index(es)*[a]	*Investment Advisor(s)*[a]
Other[b]	$ 3,609	Salomon Brothers Broad Investment-Grade Bond Index Salomon Brothers 20+ Treasury Index Lehman Brothers Government/Corporate Bond Index Lehman Brothers Long Government/Corporate Bond Index Lehman Brothers Long Government Bond Index Lehman Brothers Mortgage-Backed Securities Index	State Street Bank and Trust Company Wells Fargo Investment Advisors

Notes:

a. Investors are listed in descending size of assets, and investment advisors are listed in alphabetical order.

b. Group includes five institutions which provided the data but requested anonymity.

Appendix B

Review of Specialized Fixed Income Market Sectors

This appendix provides a summary of the different subsectors of the mortgage-backed and corporate securities markets. As described in Chapters 1 and 2, not all of these subsectors are included in broad market benchmarks.

MORTGAGE-BACKED SECURITIES[1]

Government National Mortgage Association (GNMA)

GNMA, referred to as "Ginnie Mae," is a wholly-owned U.S. Government institution within the Department of Housing and Urban Development (HUD). GNMA is responsible for two mortgage pass-through programs: GNMA I and GNMA II. Both programs consist of FHA-insured (Federal Housing Administration) or VA-guaranteed (Veterans Administration) mortgage loans and are backed by the full faith and credit of the U.S. Government. The most common

1. For an in-depth discussion of different types of mortgage-backed securities, see Frank J. Fabozzi (Editor), *The Handbook of Mortgage Backed Securities, Revised Edition*, Probus Publishing Company (Chicago, 1988).

mortgages are 30-year and 15-year maturity fixed rate level payment mortgages on single-family houses. GNMA I pools differ from GNMA II pools in that the mortgages in GNMA I pools must carry the same interest rate and must be issued by the same lender while GNMA II pools may include mortgages with a wider range of interest rates and from multiple issuers. GNMA I pools have a 15-day delay in payment of principal and interest while GNMA II pools have a 20-day delay; in addition, GNMA I pools are issued with a minimum pool size of $1 million, while GNMA II pools have a minimum requirement of $7 million. All broad market benchmarks include GNMA I pools; the Lehman Brothers Aggregate Index and the Merrill Domestic Master included GNMA II pools through the end of 1989 while the Salomon Brothers BIG Index does not include such pools.

Graduated Payment Mortgages (GPMs)

GPMs are GNMA securities issued through the GNMA I and GNMA II programs. GPMs are based on graduated payment mortgages in which part of the initial monthly payments are deferred and added to the outstanding principal; the mortgage payments, therefore, start at a relatively low level. The mortgage payments rise for a certain number of years after which they are held at a fixed level. All broad market benchmarks include GPM pass-through securities.

Mobile Home Mortgages (MH)

MH mortgages are GNMA securities issued through the GNMA I and GNMA II programs. MH pass-through securities, based on mobile (or manufactured) homes, differ from traditional GNMA mortgage pass-through securities in that the former may have a higher servicing fee (about 3.5 percent) than the normal 0.5 percent for the GNMA I program and 0.5 to 1.5 percent for the GNMA II program. MH pass-through securities are included only in the Lehman Brothers Aggregate Index and the Merrill Domestic Master.

Project Loans

FHA and GNMA project loan securities are mortgage pass-through securities or participation certificates based on HUD-insured project loans. The project loans are designed to facilitate funding primarily for low- and moderate-income family housing. FHA project loans are insured by HUD but the timely payment of principal and interest is not guaranteed. In GNMA project loans, however, the timely payment of principal and interest is guaranteed by GNMA. Most GNMA project loan securities are backed by project loans coinsured under Section 223 (f) of the National Housing Act of 1934. FHA project loans and GNMA 223 (f) project loans are included only in the Salomon Brothers BIG Index.

Federal Home Loan Mortgage Corporation (FHLMC)

FHLMC, referred to as "Freddie Mac," is a corporate institution that is owned by the Federal Home Loan Banks and member savings and loan associations. FHLMC is perceived as a quasi-agency because of its borrowing rights with the Treasury, but its guarantees are not a direct obligation of the U.S. Government. FHLMC guarantees the timely payment of interest and eventual payment of principal of FHLMC pass-through securities. FHLMC issues mortgage-backed securities primarily under two programs: a Conventional Regular PC (Participation Certificate) or Cash program and a Conventional Guarantor/Swap PC or Guarantor program. All broad market benchmarks include FHLMC mortgage-backed securities.

Federal National Mortgage Association (FNMA)

FNMA, referred to as "Fannie Mae," is also a corporate institution with quasi-agency status responsible for promoting a secondary market for single-family and multifamily mortgages. FNMA guarantees the timely payment of principal and interest for all its pass-through securities. FNMA issues mortgage-backed securities based on mortgages it purchases from originators and on a swap program similar to FHLMC's. All broad market benchmarks include FNMA mortgage-backed securities.

Private Mortgage Pass-Through Securities

Private mortgage pass-through securities are based on conventional mortgage loans issued by private mortgage originators including commercial banks, thrifts, private conduits, and home builders. Typically, these loans do not qualify for FHLMC and FNMA programs because of the large size of the loan. Private mortgage pass-through securities are not guaranteed by any government agency or quasi-agency, and therefore need some form of credit enhancement such as letters of credit, insurance, and senior-subordinated structures. Credit enhancement typically results in a AA or higher credit rating by one of the major rating agencies. None of the broad market benchmarks contain private mortgage pass-through securities.

Collateralized Mortgage Obligations (CMOs)

A CMO is a multi-class fixed income security backed by mortgage-backed securities or by a pool of whole loans. The purpose of a CMO is to use mortgage collateral with a 15-year or 30-year original maturity and with uncertain cash flows to create a series of mortgage-backed securities with different maturities and more stable cash flows. CMOs, therefore, offer the high credit quality and incremental yield of mortgage-backed securities but also offer a wide range of maturities and prepayment sensitivities. CMOs are not included in any of the broad market indexes, primarily because the underlying collateral of most CMOs is included in the indexes already.

Mortgage-Backed Bonds (MBBs)

An MBB is a debt obligation that is collateralized by mortgages. MBBs are structured to resemble corporate bonds with semi-annual interest payments and a fixed maturity date or sinking fund schedule. MBBs are overcollateralized 1) to ensure that the value of the collateral does not fall below the value of the MBBs in response to fluctuating interest rates and prepayments, and 2) to eliminate the uncertainty of cash flows and maturity date. The collateral is owned by the issuer. MBBs are included in broad market indexes as corporate bonds.

CORPORATE AND AGENCY SECURITIES

Medium Term Notes (MTNs)

MTNs are corporate or agency debentures. They differ from traditional corporate and agency securities in that they are offered on a continuous basis through an investment banker acting as agent for an issuer. A MTN program is launched after the program has been registered with the SEC, and the issuer starts posting rates for various maturity sectors. MTNs typically offer issuers and investors greater flexibility in selecting a range of coupons and maturities for their debt. MTNs also offer issuers the flexibility to issue debt at different times over the life of the MTN program to meet funding requirements. MTNs are not included in any of the broad market benchmarks, primarily because the continuous nature of the offerings and the multiple coupons and maturities of each program make it difficult to obtain and maintain the information that is required for a security's inclusion in market indexes.

Equity Contract Notes and Equity Commitment Notes (ECNs)

ECNs are mandatory convertible debt issued by bank holding companies as a low cost means of raising regulatory primary capital. The securities have a maximum maturity of 12 years and are a subordinated obligation of the bank holding company. At maturity, the principal of equity commitment notes is repaid in cash from the proceeds of the sale of primary capital securities (e.g., common stock or perpetual preferred stock) while equity contract notes may be paid directly in primary capital securities. ECNs are excluded from the Lehman Brothers Aggregate Index and Merrill Domestic Master because the source of the principal payment is equity-related.

Asset-Backed Securities (ABS)

ABS are pass-through securities backed by loans, installment contracts or leases on personal property such as credit cards, automobiles, boats, and computers. ABS are similar to mortgage-backed securities in that loans on some type of property (real estate in the case of mortgage-backed securities) are pooled into pass-through securities. Like private mortgage pass-through securities, ABS rely on letters of credit, private insurance, and senior-subordinated structures to obtain AA and AAA ratings. The first ABS was issued in 1985; however, it was not until January 1, 1990 that credit-card ABS were included in market benchmarks. A group of AAA bullet-maturity credit-card ABS are now included in the Lehman Brothers Aggregate Index as corporate securities, and all bullet-maturity credit-card ABS issued after January 1, 1989 have been included in the Salomon Brothers BIG Index since February 1, 1990. ABS backed by automobile, boat, or computer loans are not included in any broad market benchmarks.

Title XI Bonds

Title XI bonds are government-guaranteed bonds issued by U.S. shipping companies to finance the domestic construction of new U.S. ships. In order to promote the building of new ships and to support the domestic shipping industry, the U.S. Government provides a guarantee of principle and interest of Title XI bonds through the Maritime Administration. Title XI bonds have a stated interest rate and maturity date; most issues have sinking fund provisions. Title XI bonds were included in the Lehman Brothers Aggregate Index as agency securities through December 1989 and eliminated thereafter. Salomon Brothers BIG Index, too, includes Title XI bonds as agency securities.

Appendix C

Selecting an Index Fund Advisor

The criteria for selecting an index fund advisor are determined primarily by the type of indexing (pure or enhanced) desired by the investor.

PURE INDEXING

When selecting an index fund advisor for pure indexing, an investor is seeking an advisor who:

- produces the lowest realized tracking error relative to a given benchmark;
- provides portfolio reporting, market analysis, and client servicing; and
- charges the lowest advisory fees.

What is the typical screening process for choosing, from among the 50 or so index fund advisors currently available, the index fund advisor who meets these three requirements? First, a list of, say, 10 index fund advisors is compiled for further examination. The list is compiled based on several factors including advisory firm's size,

size of assets in index funds, industry reputation, and even geographic location. Such a list can be compiled by using a consultant, by relying on the trade press which often publishes data on index fund advisors, or by asking major index fund investors about their advisors (Appendix A). Information is then obtained regarding the extent to which each advisor meets the requirements outlined above. This information can be obtained directly from each advisor.

Lowest Realized Tracking Error. Identifying the index fund advisor who will produce the lowest realized tracking error requires the following information:

a. Performance history on different types and different sizes of index funds on a monthly or, at least, quarterly basis. The index fund advisor should have experience in managing the type of index fund (e.g., mortgage-backed securities, corporate, or broad market) selected by the investor.

b. Performance attribution to explain the source of any realized tracking error.

c. Description of analytical and information systems that were used to generate past performance and that will be used to maintain low realized tracking error.

d. Background of investment team associated with past performance who will be involved in future pure index funds.

Level of Service. Unlike realized tracking error which can be quantified, level of service is qualitative; moreover, different investors require different levels of service. To ascertain whether an index fund advisor will provide the required level of service, the following information should be obtained:

a. Samples of portfolio reports including transaction history, summary reports, accounting and performance reports. Frequency of each report is important.

b. Samples of broad economic reviews, market sector commentaries, and other reports used to inform clients about the fixed income market environment.

c. Level of operations support (also known as back office) to reconcile custodial statements and monitor the timeliness of payments, receipts and other transactions.

d. Frequency and type of meetings with investment advisor.

Advisory Fees. In addition to advisory fee schedules, an investor should inquire about the "negotiability" of fees for large size index funds. It is also important to know whether all clients of each index fund advisor pay a comparable fee for the same size and type of index fund.

Based on the information provided and the investor's time constraints, four or five finalists can be selected. Selecting the ideal investment advisor among the finalists will not be easy. In many instances, the finalists for pure indexing cannot be differentiated on the basis of low realized tracking error, level of service, and advisory fees. The investor must then consider additional factors. One criterion may be the extent to which an investor can rely on the index fund advisor for general fixed income research. Another criterion may be the breadth of the index fund advisor's investment resources and investment services in different asset classes. For example, one index fund advisor may have useful non-index related research reports; another may have annual conferences that will be useful to the investor in other investment-related decisions.

Ultimately the most important criterion in selecting one advisor among perhaps several equally qualified finalists may be an intangible one: the level of rapport and comfort that evolves between the investor and the index fund advisor. Meeting the finalists—preferably at the finalists' premises—is thus essential.

ENHANCED INDEXING

The initial steps for selecting an index fund advisor for enhanced indexing is similar to those used for selecting an active investment advisor.

An investor is seeking an enhanced index fund advisor who:

- produces the highest expected incremental return over the benchmark and produces such incremental return consistently and without undue risk;
- provides extensive portfolio reporting, market analysis, client service and performance attribution;
- charges advisory fees that are commensurate with the expected incremental return; and
- maintains an organizational structure that will continue to produce incremental return in a more challenging and competitive fixed income market.

Again, the first step—compiling a list of enhanced index fund advisors—is straight forward; investors can rely on a consultant, use the trade press, or ask major index fund investors about their advisors. And as with pure index fund advisors, such factors as advisory firm's size, size of assets in enhanced index funds, mix of assets between pure and enhanced index funds, industry reputation, and geographic location can be used to narrow the list of candidates to 10 or so organizations.

Each candidate then submits a proposal so that the investor can evaluate the extent to which each candidate meets the requirements for enhanced indexing.

Highest Expected Incremental Return. Some of the information required for identifying the enhanced index fund advisor with the highest expected incremental return is similar to that which is required of pure index fund advisors, notably performance history, description of analytical and information systems, and investment team associated with the index funds. Other information, however, pertains only to enhanced indexing. The enhanced index fund advisor should describe the investment strategies used to produce incremental return, and attribute past incremental return to specific strategies. Examples of past successful and unsuccessful implementations of each strategy should be provided. The enhanced index fund advisor should also explain the decision process underlying those investment strategies. The role of credit and quantitative research, in-house, broker/dealer, and third-party research, and historical and anticipated (or forecasted) data should be spelled out.

In some cases, the investor may opt for general questions, thereby enabling the candidates to highlight—in their opinion—the most critical issues. How much incremental return do you expect to provide and what strategies will you use? In other cases, the investor may opt for specific questions. How much annualized incremental return do you expect over a market cycle and what is the lowest and highest incremental return you expect in one year? What is the level of volatility required to provide such incremental return? What investment strategies do you use? How aggressive or conservative are you in implementing these strategies? What level of portfolio turnover is commensurate with your investment strategies and what is their work-out period? What is the risk of such strategies? How do you attribute incremental return to particular strategies? What explains the consistency—or lack thereof—of your past performance?

Level of Service. Most of the information regarding level of service required of enhanced index fund advisors is similar to that required of pure index fund advisors. Additional information that should be requested includes samples of performance attribution reports in different market environments.

Advisory Fees. The advisory fees for enhanced indexing are not only higher than those for pure indexing, but also less uniform. Candidates, however, should not be selected on the basis of fees alone. Investors should examine the incremental return after fees as well as the consistency of past performance. In addition, the investor should evaluate the extent to which the advisory fees provide access to other non-indexing related resources. Performance fees or higher absolute fees should also be considered for aggressively-managed enhanced index funds. Aggressively-managed enhanced index funds are not much different than actively-managed duration-controlled (or risk-controlled) funds but require more extensive analytical systems and performance attribution data; yet the fees for aggressively-managed enhanced index funds are one-half to one-third those of risk-controlled funds. In time, this pricing discrepancy will narrow.

Organizational Structure. The structure of an organization is critical to producing sustainable incremental return. Information on the history of the organization, form of ownership, business objectives, turnover of both investment, marketing, and administrative professionals, compensation and incentive systems, biographies of investment professionals, and resources supporting those investment professionals should be requested and carefully examined. The breadth and depth of the organization, and proof of commitment to future success are particularly important, given the increased complexity of, and greater competition in, the fixed income market. Finally, the candidates should demonstrate the importance of indexing to their organization.

Having narrowed the list of candidates to three or four finalists based on written proposals, the investor should then arrange for investment presentations, again preferably on the enhanced index fixed advisors' home turf. It is highly likely that the investor may be leaning already towards one or two of the finalists based on their proposals or prior experience. Selecting one enhanced index fund advisor among the finalists will be a function of the type of presentation, the response to any questions raised by the investor, the extent to which the enhanced index fund advisor can demonstrate the potential for consistent incremental return, and the chemistry established between the investor and the enhanced index fund advisor. Such final meetings can be informative, interesting, and challenging.

INTERNAL VERSUS EXTERNAL INDEX FUND ADVISORS

One of the primary advantages of internal investment management generally is lower costs. In the case of index funds—both pure and enhanced—that advantage might not in fact exist. When the size of the index fund is small—say under $300 million—the costs of internal management including information systems, analytical systems, and investment professionals is prohibitive. When the size of the index fund is very large, the investor can negotiate very favorable fees—between one and two basis points or alternatively a fixed fee for a several billion-dollar index fund. Direct costs between internal and external advisors, therefore, may be comparable. For intermediate size funds where the in-house investment professionals have other responsibilities and the broker/dealer community substitutes for in-house research and analytical systems, the direct costs may appear lower; often times, additional indirect costs exist hidden in the transaction costs incurred by trading securities with the broker/dealer community.

Internal management of index funds may prove less costly when extensive assets are managed internally with multiple investment disciplines and multiple assets classes. In such instances, the marginal cost of in-house index fund management is low. But does lower cost entail lower incremental return? For pure index funds, incremental return is not a consideration. For enhanced index funds, however, the internal advisors can be evaluated against other finalists and performance compared on the basis of consistent incremental return net of all costs.

Of course, even in such cases, the traditional arguments against internal management may still hold. For example, can internal advisors be subjected to an effective formal review process and readily terminated because of poor performance? Can one attract and retain qualified investment professionals and reward them within the compensation structure of public funds and corporations? And can one provide good career opportunities for the investment staff?

Index